D0484046

Asymmetries in U.S. and Soviet Strategic Defense Programs: Implications for Near-Term American Deployment Options

William A. Davis, Jr.

Special Report
1986

A Publication of the
INSTITUTE FOR FOREIGN POLICY ANALYSIS, INC.
Cambridge, Massachusetts, and Washington, D.C.

 PERGAMON • BRASSEY'S
International Defense Publishers

Washington New York Oxford Toronto Sydney Frankfurt

Pergamon Press Offices:

U.S.A.   Pergamon-Brassey's International Defense Publishers,
                              1340 Old Chain Bridge Road, McLean, Virginia, 22101, U.S.A.

                              Pergamon Press Inc., Maxwell House, Fairview Park,
                              Elmsford, New York 10523, U.S.A.

U.K.   Pergamon Press Ltd., Headington Hill Hall,
                              Oxford OX3 0BW, England

CANADA   Pergamon Press Canada Ltd., Suite 104, 150 Consumers Road,
                              Willowdale, Ontario M2J 1P9, Canada

AUSTRALIA   Pergamon Press (Aust.) Pty. Ltd., P.O. Box 544,
                              Potts Point, NSW 2011, Australia

FEDERAL REPUBLIC   Pergamon Press GmbH, Hammerweg 6,
OF GERMANY   D-6242 Kronberg-Taunus, Federal Republic of Germany

BRAZIL   Pergamon Editora Ltda., Rua Eça de Queiros, 346
                              CEP 04011, São Paulo, Brazil

JAPAN   Pergamon Press Ltd., 8th Floor, Matsuoka Central Building,
                              1-7-1 Nishishinjuku, Shinjuku, Tokyo 160, Japan

PEOPLE'S REPUBLIC   Pergamon Press, Qianmen Hotel, Beijing,
OF CHINA   People's Republic of China

Library of Congress Cataloging in Publication Data

Davis, William A., 1927-

    Asymmetries in U.S. and Soviet strategic defense programs.

    (Special report)
    1. Ballistic missile defenses—United States.
    2. Ballistic missile defenses—Soviet Union.
    3. Strategic Defense Initiative. I. Title. II. Series: Special report
(Institute for Foreign Policy Analysis)
UG743.D38   1986   358'.1754   86-21231

ISBN 0-08-034683-9 (pbk.)

First Printing 1986

Printed by Corporate Press, Inc., Washington, D.C.

ii

Contents

Summary Overview

Historically, the U.S. ballistic missile defense (BMD) program has cycled between periods of short-term and long-term emphasis approximately every five years. In the late 1960s, priority was given to the deployment of a system which ultimately led to the construction of a single Safeguard site. In the mid-seventies, following the signing of the ABM Treaty in 1972, there was a sharp swing toward long-term research that would not give even the appearance of a treaty violation. Then, in the early 1980s, there arose a ground swell of interest in a "quick-fix" BMD solution to U.S. land-based ICBM vulnerability. This latter interest, which focused on the LoAD/Sentry BMD system, has given way in the mid-1980s to a dominant emphasis on the long-term research goals of the Strategic Defense Initiative (SDI).

The main theme of this Special Report is that a need exists to increase the emphasis on near-term BMD development within the SDI program, while maintaining a vigorous effort to explore advanced concepts and technologies. The principal reason for this proposed shift in emphasis—toward a more balanced development program—is that the Soviets are carrying out a balanced program which includes large-scale development of near-term BMD elements, providing them with the capability for a rapid breakout from the ABM Treaty. They have not abandoned traditional BMD systems in their quest for directed-energy weapons, advanced-power systems, and other components of radically advanced BMD systems. The SDI program as presently structured is a highly effective hedge against the danger of technological surprise by the Soviets, but further emphasis is needed on near-term responsive options.

The SDI program is concentrated on the mission objective of population defense, an objective which requires high-quality, multiple tiers of defense and the employment of space-based weapons. The successful achievement of this objective would allow the transition to a strategic doctrine which reduces dependence on the threat of retaliation as a means of deterring nuclear conflict. The danger is that the SDI program will become so structured toward long-term research goals that it will not provide near-term hedge options against the ominous Soviet threats of an existent counterforce capability and an imminent capability for rapid breakout from the ABM Treaty. These threats can be met by accelerated development of systems at the traditional end of the SDI spectrum, planned as options for the initial defense of military targets. The mission of defending military targets—which are at greatest risk in the near term—is not as technically challenging as defending cities. It is therefore more feasible to develop early options for this mission.

There is unmistakable evidence that the Soviets are maintaining a near-term BMD capability, including the continued operation and upgrading of the Moscow ABM system, the development of the ABM-X-3 rapidly deployable system, and the construction of a network of early warning and tracking radars. In the latter category, the soon-to-become-operational Krasnoyarsk radar has been officially cited as a violation of the ABM Treaty, in that it is not an outward-viewing peripheral radar. There have been unconfirmed press reports that the ABM-X-3 system is being mass produced. Taken together, these developments present a chilling picture of the potential for a treaty breakout that would undermine the deterrent value of the U.S. strategic offensive forces. Such a breakout, superimposed on the present nuclear balance, would be disastrous to U.S. and allied security.

There are conflicting official and unofficial views on the objectives of SDI, particularly with regard to whether an intermediate hedge option for defense of military targets is an objective. Recently there has been increasing official tolerance for intermediate options; the SDI debate has revealed a relatively broad base of support for defending our strategic retaliatory forces. Notwithstanding the support for this type of strategic defense, there is formidable opposition to SDI in Congress and the academic community, reminiscent of the coalitions of dissent which formed during the ABM debate of the late 1960s.

This Special Report advocates a near-term hedge option that builds from the ground up—that is, one composed of traditional terminal and late midcourse defense components, which have all defensive interceptors initially based on the ground. The primary justification for this approach is that the technology for this class of BMD system is more mature. It is feasible to build such a system in the near term to defend military targets, if the need arises. It is not necessary to await the fruits of long-term SDI research—essential to the defense of cities—to meet the less demanding mission of military target defense. Moreover, an initial deployment for the latter mission can evolve efficiently toward the ultimate goal of protecting the population. In order to reduce the leadtime for a responsive option to deploy a BMD system, however, a return to prototype development is required. It is not possible to reduce deployment leadtime for a BMD system—and to close the gap with the Soviet Union—by the isolated development of subsystems. It is only through integrated development of the complete system that technical risk can be reduced, major elements balanced, and effectiveness of the system demonstrated.

The dual roles of anti-tactical ballistic missile (ATBM) and strategic missile defense can be satisfied by the same system, as the Soviets have reportedly done with their SA-X-12 system. With judicious selection of certain design features (such as interceptor velocity and radar power), a terminal BMD system can be made capable against both classes of ballistic missiles. The advantage of developing such a dual-role system is that it could be deployed in the ATBM role within the terms of the ABM Treaty, while also serving as a response option for deployment within the continental United States (CONUS). For both roles, it is prudent to conduct accelerated prototype development of a new terminal system while reserving the midcourse overlay system (the feasibility of which was demonstrated by the Homing Overlay Experiment nonnuclear kill of an ICBM warhead in June 1984) for later evolution from ongoing SDI research. This sequence is driven by the fact that the midcourse, exoatmospheric overlay components are already under development for defense against strategic missiles. Yet, except for a limit of one hundred interceptors in one CONUS site, the ABM Treaty prohibits their deployment.

The current SDI debate, like the ABM debate of the late 1960s, is marked by theological overtones that interfere with rational discourse. Much of the earlier opposition to strategic defense was couched in moralistic judgments derived from the doctrine of assured destruction; the ABM Treaty became the "bible" that codified such views. In the complex logic of assured destruction, it became dogma that strategic defense is inherently destabilizing, as it degrades the adversary's ability to destroy your own cities in a second strike. The chief architect of assured destruction, former Secretary of Defense Robert McNamara, is credited with overcoming the Soviets' instinctive resistance to banning defense of one's homeland, thereby paving the way for the ABM Treaty. Recently, some of the proponents of SDI have reversed the "holy wars," proclaiming that assured destruction is immoral and that strategic defense is inherently moral.

One troubling semantics problem related to the theological dimension of the SDI debate is the equating of "deterrence" with "assured destruction." Since everyone agrees that deterrence of nuclear conflict is preferable to any possible outcome of such a conflict, it is an advantage to claim that only one's own doctrine assures deterrence. The opponents of SDI frequently contrast strategic defense with deterrence, implying that the terms "assured destruction" and "deterrence" are synonymous. However, most supporters of SDI lay claim to the deterrent value of strategic defense, and they secondarily find comfort in the fact that should deterrence fail, some protection from the ravages of a nuclear exchange might be provided. In the words of the late Don Brennan, they prefer live Americans to dead Russians. There appears to be little constituency for a pure doctrine of "damage limitation" in the sense that it supplants deterrence and relies on counterforce capability and defense to minimize one's own damage in a nuclear exchange. But there is a growing body of strategic thought that incorporates deterrence, in a different form than that arising from assured destruction theories, into the doctrine underlying strategic defense and the SDI program.

There is a great deal of disagreement about why the Soviets acceded to the ABM Treaty, having first opposed any limitations on strategic defense. One school of thought holds that they were won over to our point of view and accepted the doctrine of assured destruction. A more plausible explanation is that they were concerned about the technology and capability embodied in the U.S. Safeguard system, and thus agreed to the ABM Treaty in order to freeze U.S. BMD technology while they played catch-up. In any event, the decade following the signing of the Treaty saw the Soviets embark on an unprecedented buildup in land-based strategic missiles—which had been set forth as a cause for abrogation of the treaty in the Jackson Amendment to Senate ratification—along with an intensive BMD development program. By contrast, the United States exercised restraint in the development of strategic offensive systems and severely curtailed even the research and development in BMD that was permitted under the Treaty. The record of Congressional budget cuts and restrictive language aimed at curtailing the BMD development program is one of overreaction to an arms control agreement and short-sightedness with respect to maintaining a technological lead. These cuts went to the extreme of prohibiting technology associated with light area defense (thin defense of cities), and not allowing prototype system development.

With the inauguration of President Reagan, the fortunes of BMD soared. Initially, the mainstream BMD system development program at the time— the LoAD/Sentry system—received greatly increased funding and priority. However, critics of LoAD/Sentry during the first year of the Reagan Administration questioned the feasibility of basing the system with MX in a deceptive basing mode. Wildly different BMD concepts were advanced, ranging from extremely primitive systems to highly exotic systems. Yet little foundation for the technical feasibility, cost, or schedule for these BMD proposals was offered, and there was no consensus on the class of system which should be pursued. After the SDI program was launched, the spectrum of systems under consideration narrowed, and the program became focused on highly advanced concepts and long-term research goals.

In addition to the fact that the technology for traditional terminal and midcourse BMD systems is more mature, the advantages of developing these systems for near-term hedge options include operational considerations. These systems can be readily applied to preferential defense of military targets, resulting in substantial savings in interceptor stockpile requirements and overall system cost. Preferential defense—while not feasible for city defense—can be exercised for military targets, if the defense is capable of sorting out where all of the attacking warheads are aimed (that is, the defense can perform accurate impact point prediction). This can be done with terminal and midcourse systems operating relatively close to the targets being defended, and employing sensors capable of tracking incoming warheads with great precision. In addition, the command and control of close-in terminal and midcourse systems can be exercised with greater confidence than that of space-based, boost-phase BMD systems where the time available for decisions is greatly compressed.

The experience of three generations of BMD systems—Safeguard, Site Defense, and LoAD/Sentry—has revealed much about the relationships between the type of development program, budget profile, and deployment leadtime. Although it is not possible to cite a definite number of years as the minimum deployment leadtime of a more or less traditional BMD system, one can bracket the range of years, depending on the type of program and the budget profile. Ideally, deployment leadtime can be reduced in a development program by about one year for every year of program funding at an optimal level for the development of tactical prototypes. For a terminal defense system of the type advocated herein (dual capability against tactical and strategic missiles), optimal funding for a period of four to five years could probably reduce leadtime to initial operational capability (IOC) to two to four years. This is not a satisfying projection of leadtime, particularly since the Soviets already have a system (the ABM-X-3) within months of an IOC. However, it is difficult to project a shorter interval based on past experience; indeed, many experienced BMD analysts would question the achievability of even this projection.

Three technical areas deserve special attention in considering a resumption of prototype development for a terminal BMD system: data processing, endoatmospheric nonnuclear kill, and discrimination. Data processing—both hardware and software—should benefit from the LoAD/Sentry concept of distributed data processing, which is generally consistent with the findings of the recent "Eastport Study" undertaken for the SDIO. In particular, it appears feasible to simplify the software by capitalizing on advancements in hardware. Endoatmospheric nonnuclear kill is the most stressing technical requirement for an advanced terminal system. While it is relatively straightforward to perform nonnuclear kill against a nonresponsive threat, the tactics of salvage fuzing and maneuvering reentry vehicles greatly complicate the task of achieving lethal intercepts. It would be prudent to develop a low-yield nuclear warhead backup, an option that appears to be politically unacceptable for ATBM application but which may be acceptable for CONUS application. Finally, discrimination—the function of differentiating between lethal warheads and penetration aids such as decoys—is the most difficult technical requirement for midcourse systems. It is relatively less stressing for terminal systems, however. There is a great deal of synergy between terminal and midcourse systems, operating with different types of sensors and profiting from dual-phenomenology discrimination techniques.

The Soviet Union has an advantage over the United States in the potential leverage of deploying a nationwide BMD system, by virtue of their existing air defense, civil defense, and space defense deployments. Ballistic missile defense is the only missing link in their defenses against strategic offensive weapons. Analyses of the results of a hypothetical nuclear exchange reveal that even a modest Soviet BMD deployment significantly reduces overall damage to their civilian and military assets. This leads to the inference that they have an incentive to break out from the ABM Treaty—or to "creep out," which some observers have suggested as a more appropriate term for what Moscow is likely to do. In addition, there is the substantial advantage of the environment in which the Soviets carry out strategic defense programs: they enjoy greater program stability to conduct research requiring many years to achieve significant results. In U.S. BMD history, changes in Administrations, in key personnel, or simply in the fads and fashions of strategic programs inflicted cutbacks or cancellations on many occasions. This is a particularly relevant problem to SDI, where the planning horizon is extremely distant.

In proposing the initiation of an accelerated prototype development program for an advanced, dual-role terminal system, one must recognize that a long-term commitment to such an initiative is necessary in order to carry it out quickly and economically. A prime contractor team competitively selected should be assigned complete responsibility for the system, under the supervision of an experienced government organization. This team must be given the resources and latitude to perform efficiently. In areas of high risk—such as endoatmospheric nonnuclear kill—there should be parallel, interactive advanced development efforts to reduce risk. Most importantly, the development team must enjoy relative autonomy and freedom of action in order to conduct this time-urgent program without the disruptions of micromanagement from higher levels of government.

1. The Current Strategic Defense Setting

Swings in BMD Emphasis

Several years ago, I composed a set of ballistic missile defense (BMD) laws, patterned after Norm Augustine's famous "laws"[1] that attempted to apply satire to some painful and ironic BMD predicaments. One of them, called "The Deserted Middle Ground," held that "there is a constituency for primitive BMD systems. There is a constituency for exotic BMD systems. There is no constituency for systems in between." At that time, I had in mind the vocal advocates of "simple, novel, low cost, rapidly deployable systems," on the one hand, and the crusaders for immediate deployment of space-based directed energy weapons on the other hand. Those of us who were officially connected with such systems as LoAD/Sentry, Midcourse Defense, and Layered Defense were caught in a no-man's-land of being either too sophisticated with our BMD system designs or too primitive. Today, the pendulum has swung toward more exotic system approaches and there is very little official or unofficial support for more traditional BMD systems.

The main theme of this monograph is that there is a need to increase the emphasis on traditional BMD development within the SDI program while maintaining a vigorous effort to explore advanced concepts and technologies. The principal reason for this proposed shift in emphasis toward a more balanced development program is that the Soviets are carrying out a balanced program, including large-scale development of near-term BMD elements, which will provide them with the capability for a rapid breakout from the ABM Treaty. They have not abandoned traditional BMD systems in their quest for directed energy weapons, advanced power systems, and other components of radically advanced BMD systems. The SDI program as presently structured is a highly effective hedge against the danger of technological surprise by the Soviet Union, but further emphasis is needed on near-term responsive options.

With the advent of the Strategic Defense Initiative (SDI), there has come an unprecedented emphasis on strategic defense which is heartily welcomed by those who were associated with BMD during its leaner years. With this emphasis has come a dominant concentration on the objective

---

[1] Norman R. Augustine, *Augustine's Laws and Major System Development Programs*, a reprint compiled from *Defense Systems Management Review* and other publications, 1980.

1

of establishing a low leakage defense of population centers using space-based weapons. There is certainly nothing wrong with this objective; in fact, those who have worked in the strategic defense community can identify with an objective that may ultimately free us from the punitive doctrine of assured destruction. The danger is that the SDI program will become so structured toward long-term research goals that it will not provide near-term hedge options against the ominous Soviet threat of an existing counterforce capability combined with an imminent capability for rapid breakout from the ABM Treaty. These threats can be met by the accelerated development of systems at the traditional end of the SDI development spectrum, designed as options for the initial defense of military targets. The mission of defending military targets, which are at greatest risk in the near term, is not as technically challenging as defending cities, and it is therefore more feasible to develop early options for this mission.

Soviet ABM Treaty Breakout Potential

Ambassador Paul Nitze recently provided an overview of the Soviet BMD program that left no doubt about its massive scale and its balanced approach to both traditional and exotic systems.[2] While he mainly addressed the Soviet research in exotic BMD technologies, many of which closely parallel SDI research initiatives, he also emphasized that their program went far beyond research. He made the important observation that Soviet military doctrine stresses that offensive and defensive forces must interact closely to achieve Soviet aims in any conflict. Consistent with that doctrine, the Soviet Union had spent, over the last two decades, roughly as much on strategic defense as it has on its massive offensive nuclear forces. He pointed to the upgrades to the deployed Moscow ABM system, which he estimated would be completed in 1987, and the new phased-array ballistic missile tracking radar near Krasnoyarsk (branded a violation of the ABM Treaty) as evidence of a potential breakout from the ABM Treaty.

Soviet Military Power, the authoritative report released each year by the Department of Defense,[3] reinforces Nitze's assessment of the Soviet Union's BMD activity and also spotlights its rapidly deployable BMD system. The 1985 edition of this report states that "The Soviets are developing a rapidly deployable ABM system to protect important areas in the USSR . . . .the Soviets could deploy such a system at sites that could be built in months

---

[2] Paul Nitze, *SDI: The Soviet Program,* United States Department of State, Bureau of Public Affairs, Current Policy No. 717, July 1985.

[3] Department of Defense, *Soviet Military Power, 1984* (Washington, D.C.: U.S. Government Printing Office, April 1984.)

instead of years." This system, designated the ABM-X-3, appears to be relatively crude, but it would be functionally effective against our ballistic missiles and it could serve particularly well as a shield against a U.S. retaliatory attack composed predominantly of SLBMs. The Krasnoyarsk radar, which, as Nitze points out, is being constructed in violation of the ABM Treaty, "closes the final gap in the combined Hen House and new large phased-array radar early warning and tracking network."[4] This ballistic missile radar network is ideally designed and located to detect and hand over targets to the ABM-X-3. Hence, all of the pieces of a "breakout" capability are falling into place. /

Even more alarming than the *Soviet Military Power* accounts of the ABM-X-3 development is a press report in 1985 that the system is being mass produced. In an editorial built around the 1985 National Intelligence Estimate 11-3-885, the *Wall Street Journal* reported that "The Soviets, despite treaty constraints, have begun mass production of a nationwide ABM-X-3 system, according to 11-3-885."[5] The authenticity of this report cannot be automatically assumed, but the Soviet disregard for the ABM Treaty in other areas leaves little room for complacency.

Policy Emphasis on Long-Term Research

If there is an asymmetry in U.S. and Soviet capabilities to deploy a BMD system in the near term, there is also the troubling question of how this condition relates to U.S. strategic policy. Congressman Les Aspin, Chairman of the House Armed Services Committee, has raised this question, along with a number of other spokesmen who express varying degrees of enthusiasm for SDI.[6] Congressman Aspin asked whether SDI is a population defense system to replace deterrence, or a military target defense system that will enhance deterrence. He pointed out that much testimony before his committee indicated that defense of the strategic deterrent force was more feasible than population defense and could, therefore, be realized in an earlier timeframe. In fact, he expressed some skepticism that population defense could ever be achieved.

If we scan the record to answer Congressman Aspin's questions, we encounter persistent ambiguities. There appears, however, to be growing support for near-term options for the defense of military targets. The

---

[4] Department of Defense, *Soviet Military Power, 1985* (Washington, D.C.: U.S. Government Printing Office, April 1985.)

[5] *Wall Street Journal*, Editorial, "Winnable Nuclear War," July 16, 1985.

[6] Representative Les Aspin, Chairman, House Armed Services Committee, address to a Carnegie Endowment luncheon in Washington, D.C., January 17, 1985, quoted in *Aerospace Daily*, January 22, 1985.

problem is that the initial announcement of SDI, about three years ago, set in motion institutional forces that cast the program as a long-term enterprise; thus, more recent expressions of interest in intermediate objectives cannot be readily implemented because of the momentum of the program. There are both official indications and informal "working level" signs that this dichotomy between evolving policy and program content is real and that it is creating credibility problems for the program.

There can be little doubt that President Reagan's dramatic announcement of SDI, on March 23, 1983, was intended to launch a long-term quest for a near-impenetrable defense of the nation against ballistic missiles. His words—"destroy ballistic missiles before they reached our own soil or that of our allies . . . . I know this is a formidable technical task, one that may not be accomplished before the end of this century. . . . I am directing a comprehensive and intensive effort to define a long-term research and development program to begin to achieve our ultimate goal of eliminating the threat posed by strategic nuclear missiles. . . . "[7]—established this context.

In a speech on March 29, 1985, President Reagan was even more explicit about his preference for a long-term defensive shield instead of an interim defense of military targets. He said:

Now, this is not and should never be misconstrued as just another method of protecting missile silos. . . .

. . . The means to intercept ballistic missiles during their early-on boost phase of trajectory would enable us fundamentally to change our strategic assumptions, permitting us to shift our emphasis from offense to defense.

. . . We're not discussing a concept just to enhance deterrence, but rather a new kind of deterrence; not just an addition to our offensive forces, but research to determine the feasibility of a comprehensive nonnuclear defensive system—a shield that could prevent nuclear weapons from reaching their targets.[8]

In the same vein, Dr. George Keyworth, then the President's Science Adviser, in a speech on March 29, 1985, posed the question: "Is the SDI the means to protect people or to protect weapons?"[9] He went on to answer that it is not only to protect people, but that those who suggest it be considered for protecting weapons do a disservice to the program. He recited three main tenets being advanced by those who would deflect the SDI program from its true goal: "strengthening deterrence," according

---

[7] U.S. Congress, Office of Technology Assessment, *Ballistic Missile Defense Technologies*, OTA-ISC-254 (Washington, D.C.: U.S. Government Printing Office, September 1985), Appendix H.

[8] Ibid.

[9] Ibid.

4

to them, should be the main goal; protecting weapons, especially ICBM silos, is the nearer-term and most likely goal; ATBM for European military targets is the most politically attractive near-term goal. He concluded that if these arguments continue to be used for political expediency, the President's objective of strategic change will be lost forever.

This series of statements is consistent and unequivocal in its insistence on a long-range program designed to achieve the capability for population defense and to avoid any diversions toward near-term goals for military target defense. Yet, in excerpts from other official statements, presented below, an equally compelling case is made that near-term defense goals are part and parcel of SDI. It should be noted there is no chronological consistency to the various statements that have been made; there is no basis to conclude that a change in policy began to take place at some point in time and that clarifying statements were consistent following that change. However, before presenting the "other side" of official policy, it is worth noting how the machinery of government at the lower echelons reacted and responded to the initial SDI guidance.

Translation of Policy Into Program

The Defense Technology Study Team (DTST), or Fletcher Panel, which was convened following the President's March 23, 1983 speech to lay out an implementing technology plan for SDI, had "marching orders" to emphasize long-term concepts and to abandon traditional BMD systems. As frequently happens when a high-level charter is handed down, most of the Fletcher Panel participants tended to amplify the direction given, and proceeded to structure a plan which was extremely futuristic. Very little attention was given to the fruits of thirty years of prior BMD research and development, and there was a perceptible avoidance of the incremental, evolutionary approach to development of BMD technologies and systems. The product of DTST was a blueprint for a giant leap toward the ultimate strategic defense objective of population defense.

The DTST study was integrated into the SDI program and organization and became institutionalized, almost to the point of a verbatim translation of the study findings and report sections into program elements. As time went by, the program took on rigidities that have resisted the increasing pressures for adapting and responding to current exigencies. Now, three years into the program, many experienced BMD engineers at the working level realize that program elements are too stretched out, technology milestones are too ambitious to schedule confidently, and, in general, the program is too protracted to "get a handle" on planning for defense applications.

5

The direct and pervasive influence of the DTST study on the formulation of the SDI program was in stark contrast to the impact of a parallel policy study conducted by Fred Hoffman.[10] This study reached conclusions which were nearly opposite from those of the DTST study, and they seemed to lie fallow until recent official statements began to swing in their direction. The main theme of the Hoffman Report is that "a flexible research and development (R&D) program for the deployment of intermediate systems, while proceeding toward the President's ultimate goal, is preferable to one that defers the availability of components having a shorter development leadtime in order to optimize the allocation of R&D resources for development of the 'full system.' "[11] In support of the development of a U.S. near-term BMD hedge option, this study stressed the view that a Soviet ABM Treaty breakout, superimposed on the present nuclear balance, would be disastrous to U.S. and allied security.

Shift Toward Intermediate Options

Secretary of Defense Caspar Weinberger appeared to make a pronounced policy shift in a speech on December 19, 1984. If it were not for subsequent official statements, cited above, that reverted to the theme of exclusive concentration on long-term research, it could be inferred that the Hoffman Report's incremental approach had gained ascendancy. The following excerpts from this speech convey an unmistakable change in tone from earlier pronouncements:

We all recognized from the outset that a complete system, or combination of systems, for strategic defenses could not be deployed overnight. There could be a transitional period when some defenses would be deployed and operating before others would be ready. . . . If properly planned and phased, the transitional capabilities would strengthen our present deterrent capability, which is one of President Reagan's high priorities. In fact, they could make a major contribution to the prevention of nuclear war, even before a fully effective system is deployed.

If the Soviet leaders ever contemplated initiating a nuclear attack, their purpose would be to destroy U.S. or NATO military forces that would be able to oppose the aggression. Defenses that could deny the Soviet missiles the military objectives of their attack, or deny the Soviets confidence in the achievement of those objectives, would discourage them from even considering such an attack, and thus be a highly effective deterrent.[12]

The official tolerance for intermediate BMD deployment options has been picked up and amplified by many writers and spokesmen in the SDI

---

[10] Fred S. Hoffman, Study Director, *Ballistic Missile Defenses and U.S. National Security*, Summary Report, prepared for the Future Security Strategy Study, October 1983.

[11] Ibid.

[12] Caspar W. Weinberger, "The Rationale for Strategic Defense," speech to the Foreign Press Center in Washington, D.C., on December 19, 1984, printed in *Wall Street Journal*, January 2, 1985.

debate. As an example, there was a popular article in the *New York Times* Magazine that proposed a two-step BMD deployment, with emphasis on initial protection of our strategic deterrent forces. Its authors, Zbigniew Brzezinski, Robert Jastrow, and Max M. Kampelman, underscored the urgency of a near-term deployment option by describing the Soviet first-strike weapons and the resulting vulnerability of our "missiles, the Strategic Air Command and nuclear submarine bases."[13] They presented a scenario of a multiple Soviet strike capability, using their reloadable missiles, and the dismal prospect that the American President might be forced to make important political concessions in order to avoid catastrophe. Against this background, they presented the technical, strategic and political arguments in favor of an evolutionary strategic defense deployment.

Jastrow has been a prolific and effective advocate of SDI in many different forums and media. His demolition of the flawed criticism of SDI espoused by the Union of Concerned Scientists (UCS) is perhaps his greatest contribution to reason and sanity in the debate.[14] His work has found its way into publications likely to be widely read by the American public. His thesis about SDI was simply stated in a recent article which merits the thoughtful consideration of participants in the debate as well as the informed layman. At base, what he has to say is consistent with the premises and arguments of this Special Report and, therefore, I will paraphrase his main points.

Jastrow states with clarity and force that the Soviet Union has created a massive nuclear stockpile that is designed for the destruction of the United States, rather than as a deterrent to an attack on the USSR. He strips away all ambiguity and enfeebling doubts about what the Soviet forces are designed to threaten, and therefore what we need to defend: They seek "to destroy the missile silos and other military installations of the United States and cripple our power to retaliate against a Soviet attack." He then stresses the need to support SDI as a means of defending our retaliatory forces, with an accelerated deployment option for the early 1990s, to restore the credibility of deterrence. With the dire assessment that the Soviet threat to our deterrent force constitutes the greatest peril our nation has ever known, Jastrow comes very close to warning that if we do not create a near-term option for the defense of military targets we may not survive long enough to develop the ultimate capability for population defense.[15]

---

[13] Zbigniew Brzezinski, Robert Jastrow, and Max M. Kampelman, "Defense in Space Is Not 'Star Wars,' " *New York Times* Magazine, January 27, 1985.

[14] Robert Jastrow, "The War Against 'Star Wars,' " *Commentary*, December 1984.

[15] Robert Jastrow, "Why We Need 'Star Wars,' " *Reader's Digest*, February 1986.

Perhaps the most authoritative recognition of the problem of leadtimes and related research priorities within SDI came from the U.S. Senate. The following words from the Senate Armed Services Committee, in its Fiscal Year 1986 Authorization Bill, express the problem succinctly:

> . . .the committee is concerned that the Strategic Defense Initiative Organization (SDIO) is placing insufficient emphasis on near-term (within 10 years) defensive deployment options. On the basis of testimony received from public witnesses, the committee believes that a higher priority should be assigned to research on near-term deployment options. . . .[16]

The Range of SDI Criticism

Critics of SDI appear to be less concerned about the defense of military targets than they are about the defense of cities. This stems from both doctrinal and technical feasibility reasons. Defense of military targets does less violence to the doctrine of assured destruction, and it is less difficult to perform from a technology standpoint. As an example of the latter consideration, Harold Brown flatly asserts that "technology does not offer even a reasonable prospect of a successful population defense," but adds that "An ABM defense with this more limited purpose of defending land-based missiles could be accomplished through a terminal defense and is feasible with known technology. Space-based weapons would probably not be cost effective as part of such an ABM system, though space-based sensors could be." Brown avers that there is no need to pursue defensive systems for the objective of defending land-based missiles because the threat of vulnerability does not exist today and is "not likely to arise during this century if the U.S. pursues a strategic modernization program."[17]

Ashton Carter, who has a background of relatively moderate and objective views on traditional BMD systems, created a storm of official reaction with his sweeping observation: "The prospect that emerging 'Star Wars' technologies, when further developed, will provide a perfect or near-perfect defense system . . . is so remote that it should not serve as the basis of public expectation or national policy about ballistic missile defense (BMD)." He went on to add that "For modest defensive goals requiring less-than-perfect performance, traditional reentry phase defenses and/or more advanced midcourse defenses might suffice."[18]

---

[16] FY 86 Senate Armed Services Committee Report, *Congressional Record*, pp. 166-168.

[17] Harold Brown, "The Strategic Defense Initiative: Defensive Systems and the Strategic Debate," The Foreign Policy Institute, School of Advanced International Studies, The Johns Hopkins University, December 14, 1984.

[18] Ashton B. Carter, "Directed Energy Missile Defense in Space," Background Paper prepared under contract for the Office of Technology Assessment, April 1984.

Richard Garwin has been a conspicuous critic of SDI, in association with the Union of Concerned Scientists and in many other channels of the current debate. Over the years, he has been a dependable foe of any form of BMD which appears to be emerging as a serious government program. I can recall briefing him in 1969 on the Minuteman Defense Study, Phase I. At that time he expressed a preference for the newer, smaller defense system coming out of that study over the Safeguard system. Later, he showed more support for the LoAD/Sentry system than for the Site Defense system which sprang from the earlier Minuteman Defense Studies. However, during the LoAD/Sentry era, he invented a host of "simple, rapidly deployable and low-cost BMD systems" which he advocated for defense of our land-based missiles. Among these were his "bed of nails" concept for impaling attacking warheads with spikes implanted in the ground around our land-based missiles, and "environmental defense" which entailed the difficult political decision to detonate nuclear devices at or near our missile fields in order to kill attacking warheads by collision with the resulting debris. His record, then, is not one of opposing any and all forms of BMD, but one of concentrating his attack on the highest profile version of BMD coming out of the Pentagon and advocating his own BMD system designs. Recently, in collaboration with other scientists, Garwin expressed "complete agreement" with Ashton Carter's sweeping indictment of SDI.[19]

A revealing insight into the ambivalence some SDI critics have about ground-based BMD for military targets versus space-based BMD for cities can be gained by reading Charles Krauthammer. He followed a particularly negative piece on SDI in 1984 with a sequel in 1985 that contained these concessions to BMD:

Writing about Star Wars last year ("The Illusion of Star Wars," TNR, May 14, 1984), I concluded that instead of a ruinous arms race in space that could never hope to achieve its objectives, a better alternative was arms control ("perhaps augmented by improved terminal defenses to protect missile bases and enhance deterrence. . . .") . . . A partial American defense around (military) targets, even a leaky one, would, in effect and unilaterally, degrade this Soviet arsenal. It would close the famous window of vulnerability proclaimed by Ronald Reagan and others in the 1970s.[20]

As a benchmark, it should be recorded that there are critics of SDI who are not ambivalent, whose opinions are not clouded by doubts or diluted with exceptions, but who strongly condemn the program. Such is the case with four famous Americans who have sometimes been referred to

---

[19] Hans A. Bethe, Richard L. Garwin, Kurt Gottfried, and Henry W. Kendall, "Space-Based Ballistic Missile Defense," *Scientific American*, October 1984.
[20] Charles Krauthammer, "Will Star Wars Kill Arms Control?," *New Republic*, January 21, 1985.

as the "gang of four" since their collaboration on the definitive castigation of SDI. McGeorge Bundy, George F. Kennan, Robert S. McNamara, and Gerard Smith cast these invectives against SDI:

What is centrally and fundamentally wrong with the President's objective is that it cannot be achieved. . . . It will destroy the Anti-Ballistic Missile (ABM) Treaty . . .; it will directly stimulate both offensive and defensive systems on the Soviet side; and as long as it continues it will darken the prospect for significant improvement in the currently frigid relations between Moscow and Washington. . . . the President has repeatedly proposed a solution that combines surface plausibility and intrinsic absurdity in a way that tells a lot about what is wrong with Star Wars itself. . . . This has not been a cheerful analysis. . . .[21]

Building from the Ground Up

It has not been my objective, in reciting the foregoing conflicting views and contradictory statements about SDI from both official and unofficial sources, to denigrate the program. I have presumed that the current debate has room for a believer in SDI who thinks that the program needs a shift in emphasis. At the same time, I am mindful of the polarization of views in the debate and the difficulty of presenting constructive criticism that will not be taken out of context or construed as anti-SDI rhetoric. During the brief three-year history of the program, I have tracked its formation and direction with a range of reactions that evolved from unmitigated enthusiasm at the outset to genuine concern about its rigid concentration on the far horizons. In sifting through the welter of SDI literature and commentary, I have been heartened by the increasing expressions of support for a near-term BMD segment in the program to provide a prudent hedge option for the defense of our retaliatory forces. On the other hand, I have been close enough to the program to see conclusive and depressing evidence that it simply cannot support such an option as presently structured. Fortunately, this is not a fatal flaw; a practical and implementable reorientation of the program can infuse this option without giving up its salutary long-term goals.

What kind of system must be developed to achieve a near-term deployment option? Unfortunately, this question is answered in many conflicting and confusing ways in the current SDI debate. There are some who imply that the SDI program, as presently constituted, can more or less automatically spin off intermediate systems as it marches toward the ultimate system. This view exposes a lack of appreciation of crucial BMD system development principles and/or a misunderstanding of the content of the current SDI program. There are others who imply that the old, traditional systems, such as LoAD/Sentry, are lying there on the shelf ready to be

---

[21] McGeorge Bundy, George F. Kennan, Robert S. McNamara, and Gerard Smith, "The President's Choice: Star Wars or Arms Control," *Foreign Affairs*, Winter 1984/85.

picked up, if necessary, for immediate deployment. Again, this is a mistaken view of the realities of BMD system development, especially with respect to the perishability of system designs and the erosion of the required industrial base. There are even those who suggest that space-based weapons can be considered for near-term deployment. Later, we will discuss the problem of developing space-based weapons for near-term defense of military targets, but for now it should suffice to note that not even the most optimistic official statement on SDI has hinted that this class of weapon can be fielded in the near term.

It is unfashionable, especially among the troglodytes of past BMD programs, to suggest a retreat to the relatively unglamorous domain of traditional BMD systems. Often overlooked by those who express disdain for traditional BMD systems is the enormous importance of what is being defended. While it is technically justifiable to seek long-term, advanced technologies for performing the challenging mission of city defense, it does not follow that exotic technologies and systems are required for the defense of military targets. In fact, a compelling case can be made that traditional systems, capable of exercising preferential defense firing doctrines and making use of close-in battlespace by virtue of target hardness, are ideal for military targets such as ICBM silos.

The kind of system that is needed, then, is a two-layer defense system, composed of conventional late midcourse and terminal defense elements, with all of the interceptors based on the ground. These two complementary systems are of relatively low technical risk—the late midcourse part being an extrapolation of the successful Homing Overlay Experiment (HOE), which successfully demonstrated the exoatmospheric nonnuclear kill of an ICBM warhead in June 1984; and the terminal part being similar to the design features of LoAD/Sentry. Some of these elements are already under development in the SDI program, but they need to be integrated into a tightly defined layered system with centralized control of the system configuration. Following system baselining, the terminal defense part of a layered defense system should be broken out for accelerated prototype development.

As will later be discussed, the terminal defense system should be prototype-developed as an ATBM system so as to allow its deployment in NATO under the terms of the ABM Treaty. The main components of such a system—a high acceleration nonnuclear interceptor (preferably with a back-up nuclear warhead option) and a mobile phased-array radar—are not so far along in current SDI studies that they could not be preserved as treaty-compliant, ATBM components. (It is not equally clear that the midcourse components of the system could be so designated, since they

11

are already under development.) Such a terminal defense prototype system would constitute a counterpart to the Soviet SA-X-12 ATBM system, and would possess similar capability against strategic ballistic missiles. In addition to its utility for defense of critical NATO targets against tactical ballistic missiles, it would serve as the rapidly deployable hedge option for the defense of key military targets in the continental United States (CONUS). The late midcourse overlay could come along later to strengthen the defense, and other elements of SDI could evolve to create ultimately the full SDI system currently envisioned.

This is not to suggest that the United States break out from the ABM Treaty and deploy a system in the continental United States. Even though the Soviets have violated the Treaty with their Krasnoyarsk radar deployment, there does not appear to be sufficient justification at this time to warrant a full-scale U.S. deployment in response. Therefore, I am led to the conclusion that it would be prudent to accelerate development of a terminal defense system which could be deployed in NATO, and which could also be rapidly deployed in CONUS in response to a Soviet breakout.

Return to Terminal System Prototyping

The key difference between what I have suggested above and what is happening now in the SDI program is my greater emphasis on prototype development of a terminal defense system. Prototyping is required to reduce deployment leadtime. If the current Soviet advantage in BMD deployment leadtime is to be overcome, it must be done by system prototype development. It cannot be achieved by exploratory development of exotic components and isolated development of advanced BMD subsystems.

Dr. Edward Teller, sometimes credited with influencing President Reagan to launch the Strategic Defense Initiative, is a strong advocate of developing an early terminal defense system. Moreover, he understands the advantages of pursuing a terminal system for the near term in preference to space-based weapons. The following quotations are pertinent:

There is one special area in defense on which we have made real progress, although not yet enough; that is terminal defense. After the atmosphere has filtered out the light decoys and only the expensive, heavy missile can penetrate, there is still time to react, particularly if we have early warning.

Only one defense component in space is really necessary: observation satellites. These are not necessarily battle stations. Battle stations are expensive to deploy, inexpensive to shoot down, and, therefore, at present I have my doubts as to their value.

12

. . . Terminal defense, and thereby for the time being, the defense of our retaliatory force, is something real, something on which we can make a beginning.[22]

Needed: A Shift But Not a Major Swing

The situation in strategic defense today, then, is one of a massive U.S. program that has geared up to pursue the ultimate system and, in the process, has de-emphasized the incremental gains in technology and tightly controlled system prototyping required for realistic early hedge options. On the other hand, the Soviet Union is pursuing a balanced program that encompasses near-term systems and long-term research goals. We have no counterparts to their upgraded Moscow ABM system, their network of battle management radars, their ABM-X-3 rapidly deployable system, or their SA-X-12 ATBM system. The answer is not to abandon long-term research goals, vital to the ultimate achievement of high quality defense, but to tighten up the integration of a layered late midcourse/terminal defense system and to initiate prototype development of a terminal defense system.

The achievement of a reasonable balance in the BMD program is an admittedly difficult goal. I can remember a situation that existed in the Safeguard era of the U.S. BMD program just the opposite of that which prevails today in the SDI program. At that time, near-term effort was dominant and long-term research was an obscure part of the total program. Reflection on the imbalance of that era makes it easier to understand why some people today are concerned about any diminution of the SDI emphasis on long-term research. The state of U.S. BMD technology was more or less frozen into the Safeguard design and the rate of progress on new concepts and advanced technology was severely limited by a low priority and a small budget.

During this period, there was concern in the Pentagon that the Safeguard budget demands might lead to a siphoning off of even the modest investment then being applied to BMD advanced technology. To prevent this from happening, the Advanced Ballistic Missile Defense Agency (ABMDA) was created as a separate BMD organization, and its budget was "fenced." These measures succeeded in protecting a small effort in advanced technology, but it was clearly a period when deployment commitment dominated the BMD world and bold technology advances were not the order of the day. Certainly, we should not return to that kind of BMD program today. Although it seems to be a very remote possibility, any shift in emphasis of the SDI program toward the near term should be

---

[22] Edward Teller, speech at United States Space Foundation Symposium, "Space: The Next Ten Years," Colorado Springs, November 26-28, 1984.

13

accompanied by safeguards to prevent undue distraction from its long-term research objectives.

In the following chapters of this study, the theme of a balanced BMD program, containing a vigorous near-term prototype development segment, will be further developed, in the context of the current SDI debate, the ABM Treaty, the history of the BMD program prior to SDI, and fundamental BMD system principles and technology requirements. Chapter 2 will treat theology, doctrine, and politics in strategic defense; Chapter 3 will discuss BMD systems and technology; and Chapter 4 will contrast the strategic environment in the United States and the Soviet Union in terms of its effects on BMD program stability and operational effectiveness.

2. Theology, Doctrine, and Politics

Theological Schools and Moral Arguments

Strategic defense has the peculiar property of invoking religious fervor, both for and against its development and use, far more than other defense programs. One of the most vivid recollections I have of joining the Army's ballistic missile defense program in the late 1960s is the intensity of the emotions surrounding the "ABM Debate" of that period. I could not fathom then, and I cannot today, how a purely benign defensive system could be cast in the role of a destabilizing agent and the "rogue elephant" defense program of all time. As I watched the academic community rise up in arms against BMD and witnessed the fiery town meetings in New England protesting BMD components being built in their backyard, I wondered why protection against the devastation of nuclear ballistic missiles was more hated and feared than the ballistic missiles themselves.

I gradually began to learn the reasons for the opposition against BMD, wrapped up in the abstruse theory of assured destruction, but I could never give intellectual assent to those reasons. Senator Moynihan has written, with characteristic bluntness:

I had best be out with it directly. Deterrence was a stunning intellectual achievement. It "solved" the seemingly insoluble problem of how to control the use of nuclear weapons. But it was flawed and has been undone by the intuitive but wrong assumption that the Soviets would see the logic of our solution and do as we did. Especially that they would see the meaninglessness of strategic "superiority."[23]

I have learned that the "tablets" upon which the holy writ of anti-BMD dogma is chiseled were supplied by the ABM Treaty. This Treaty, signed in May 1972, has been glaringly ineffective in arresting arms buildups, but that deficiency has never diminished its sacredness to believers in assured destruction and opponents of BMD. It is a solitary monument to the strategic systems arms control process of the past generation, and it casts an almost mystical spell over its idolaters. The strength of its influence first struck me when members of the Congress, in the 1970s, spoke of the "spirit" of the Treaty in defending their budget cuts of BMD R&D, even though such R&D was completely compliant with the Treaty and the Soviet Union was going all out in its BMD development efforts.

---

[23] Daniel Patrick Moynihan, "The SALT Process," Reflections, *The New Yorker*, November 19, 1979.

John Newhouse has elevated the description of religious schools of thought in the strategic world to an unparalleled level of scholarship and irony. In discussing the strategic theologies leading up to SALT I and the ABM Treaty, he has this to say:

> This structure is to the metaphysics of deterrence what the post-Nicaean fathers of the Church—the Scholastics, say—were to Christian theology. So much of the substance and vocabulary of SALT are at least as remote from reality, as most of us perceive it, as early Christian exegesis. . . . As in the case of the early Church, contending schools form around antagonistic strategic concepts. The most relevant of these are known as assured destruction and damage limitation, and each can claim broad support and intellectual respectability. Debates between the two schools recall those between the Thomists and the essentially Franciscan followers of Duns Scotus. The Thomists prevailed, as have the proponents of assured destruction, who assert, for example, that ballistic-missile defense of population is immoral because it may degrade your adversary's ability to destroy your own cities in a second strike. . . .[24]

So, there it is in black and white, an authoritative statement informing us that proponents of assured destruction assert that the defense of populations against nuclear attack is immoral! And why is it immoral? Because it degrades your adversary's ability to destroy your own cities in a second strike. Here is the elusive reason for the antagonism toward BMD in the late 1960s; here is the theological underpinning to the mystifying antipathy toward "saving lives rather than avenging them." By extension, it is also the reason why the Congress was hostile toward any form of BMD in the years immediately following the signing of the ABM Treaty. However, much of the original logic was lost in the extension. The Congress opposed R&D for defense of ICBM silos in the early 1970s, a program designed to enhance assured destruction, almost as vehemently as they opposed defense of population.

Interestingly, Newhouse's reference to BMD being immoral in the eyes of the proponents of assured destruction has a modern-day parallel in the rhetoric of some advocates of the President's SDI program. Now, criticism is heard from some of the proponents of SDI that assured destruction is immoral precisely because it does not seek to protect our citizens, and instead threatens to launch nuclear ballistic missiles against enemy cities in retaliation for an attack against the United States. Perhaps the most provocative expression of this criticism was the television commercial featuring the little girl peering out her window at the stars with the clear message that "Star Wars" would protect her life but assured destruction would risk it. This turning of the tables in the "holy wars" has caused many of the assured destruction adherents to respond with emotions ranging from righteous indignation to unbridled rage. Former Sec-

---

[24] John Newhouse, *Cold Dawn: The Story of SALT* (New York: Holt, Rinehart and Winston, 1973), p. 9.

retary of Defense James R. Schlesinger perhaps speaks with the most carefully measured words for this group:

In the follow-up to the President's speech a rather loose rhetoric developed within the Administration in which the most fervent supporters of the SDI began to speak of *the immorality of deterrence.* Let me make this admonition clear. Within the Air Force, within the Administration, and within the society as a whole, the justification for strategic defense should never be based on assertions regarding the "immorality" of deterrence. For the balance of our days the security of the Western world will continue to rest on deterrence. Those were—and are—reckless words.[25]

In his recent book, Keith Payne has treated the moral issues surrounding SDI in a most comprehensive and even-handed manner.[26] He centers his discussion on the American Conference of Catholic Bishops' pastoral letter of May 3, 1983. He explains that the pastoral letter makes general and specific recommendations concerning the character of a strategic policy that is compatible with the moral standard of the "just war" tradition, but it does not endorse deployment of BMD. He notes that the letter is supportive of research and study of the feasibility of strategic defense, but it proposes other long-term approaches to find a solution to the nuclear threat. He raises the question of whether the bishops' alternative long-term approach of disarmament and a new world order are realistic and therefore preferable to strategic defense.

Semantics Sin: Deterrence = Assured Destruction

One of the great sources of confusion in the current debate, reflected in the above quotations of Secretary Schlesinger and Senator Moynihan, is the ambiguity of the terms "deterrence" and "assured destruction." They are frequently used interchangeably. Yet they are not synonymous terms. "Deterrence" should not, on theoretical or practical grounds, be the sole preserve of the doctrine of "assured destruction"; it is a broader term that can legitimately be claimed as both an objective and end result of strategic defense. Strategic defense can contribute to deterrence in a different way than assured destruction. Whether it is the "ultimate" defense of population, or an interim defense of strategic military targets, it can deter attack by creating uncertainty in the attacker's mind about the potential success of an attack. "Assured destruction" deters by the threat of retaliation; strategic defense deters by creating uncertainty. Therefore, in order to be semantically correct, the supporters of SDI should not speak of the

---

[25] James R. Schlesinger, "SDI: The Quintessential Bargaining Chip," *Aerospace America,* July 1985, p. 51. This article is derived from a speech made at the 1984 National Security Issues Symposium.

[26] Keith B. Payne, *Strategic Defense: "Star Wars" in Perspective* (Lanham, Md.: Hamilton Press, 1986).

"immorality of deterrence," since deterrence is a shared objective; rather, they should speak of the "immorality of assured destruction," which embodies the moral choice which disturbs them (assuming, of course, that a moral argument is proper in the first place).

I suppose there are purists in the debate who believe in "damage limitation" as opposed to "assured destruction," in keeping with the clean distinctions of Newhouse's religious analogy. However, "damage limitation," in its most literal interpretation, connotes an insensitivity to the "no win" horrors of a nuclear exchange; it implies an attitude of "I will not try to deter nuclear attack; I will instead limit my losses when the inevitable occurs." I would observe that most believers in strategic defense, and the majority of supporters of SDI, are not first and foremost adherents of pure "damage limitation" as an abstract doctrine. They lay claim to the deterrent value of strategic defense; what comfort they find in the fact that, should deterrence fail, they might have some protection from the ravages of a nuclear exchange is of secondary importance. Furthermore, they prefer this state of affairs to one in which the only response to the failure of deterrence is to retaliate. To borrow from the vivid language of the late Donald Brennan, believers in strategic defense are more concerned about live Americans than dead Russians.

One of the best known modern-day apostles of assured destruction, and an egregious purveyor of the careless terminology noted above, is the writer Strobe Talbott. The following excerpt from an essay in *Time* magazine serves as a good example of the semantic transgressions I have discussed and as a transition to more thoughtful opinion on the doctrinal implications of strategic defense:

It has long been part of the dogma of the nuclear age that the best defense is a good offense. That is what deterrence is all about: the other side is less likely to attack if its leaders know they will prompt a vastly destructive counterattack. A corollary to the dogma of "offense-dominated" deterrence is that there is nothing more provocative and destabilizing than a strategic defense. The more one superpower tries to protect itself against attack, the more the other side will try to improve its offensive weapons to be sure it can overwhelm and thwart those defenses. Thus a defensive arms race will exacerbate and accelerate the offensive one, with the advantage always remaining with the offense.[27]

Colin Gray has responded effectively to the "bumper sticker" logic expressed here by Talbott. Gray's target was the then-Chairman of the Democratic National Committee, Charles Manatt. Mr. Manatt had used intemperate language against the President's SDI, charging that it represented a commitment to "propel America through a dangerous threshold toward war in space" and that it would be so provocative that "it could

---

[27] Strobe Talbott, "The Case Against Star Wars Weapons," *Time*, May 7, 1984.

risk preemptive attack." Interestingly, Manatt also used the same slogans as Talbott, that "deterrence means the best defense is a good offense" and "defensive weapons are inherently destabilizing and are the greatest source of strategic provocation." Colin Gray responded:

> As a university teacher of strategic theory I must say that I would flunk Mr. Manatt. For his benefit let me say that states have offensive and defensive goals, and the U.S. strategic defenses capable, or believed to be capable, of thwarting Soviet offensive goals, may deter just as reliably—and rather more safely—than U.S. offensive retaliatory forces capable of thwarting Soviet defensive goals. . . . The doctrinal opposition to the SDI that we hear today is a cry from the past and will come to be seen as being functionally analogous to the arguments of the surface Navy against airpower, and of horse-minded cavalry men against mechanization. Those people were sincere, could appeal to the professional experience of their lifetime, and *they were wrong.*[28]

There is at least one recorded case where a celebrated American admitted that he was wrong in placing such blind faith in the religious tenets of assured destruction. In a speech in Brussels on September 1, 1979, former Secretary of State Henry A. Kissinger said:

> Since the middle of the 1960s the growth of the Soviet force has been massive. . . . And the amazing phenomenon about which historians will ponder is that all of this has happened without the United States attempting to make a significant effort to rectify that state of affairs. One reason was that it was not easy to rectify. But another reason was the growth of a school of thought to which I, myself, contributed . . . which considered that strategic stability was a military asset in which the amazing theory developed, i.e., historically amazing, that vulnerability contributed to peace and invulnerability contributed to the risks of war. . . . It cannot have occurred often in history that it was considered an advantageous military doctrine to make your own country deliberately vulnerable. I repeat, I contributed myself to some of the theories and thus I am not casting blame here on any particular group (because everyone here who knows me knows that the acceptance of blame is not the attribute for which I will go down in history). . . .[29]

I believe that it is safe to assume, from the above confession and other more recent supportive statements about SDI, that Mr. Kissinger no longer subscribes to the notion that deterrence is exclusively or ideally provided by assured destruction.

One of the most scholarly and illuminating treatments of the knotty relationships between strategic defense, deterrence, and assured destruction was provided by the Australian strategist, Desmond Ball. He argues that assured destruction "is only the 'very essence' of one particular formulation of the deterrence concept and then, it is far from the whole essence. It has never been an appropriate characterization of U.S. strategic policy."

---

[28] Colin S. Gray, "Space and National Security," luncheon address before the 3rd Annual Military Space Symposium of the American Astronautical Society, June 21, 1984.

[29] Henry A. Kissinger, "NATO: The Next Thirty Years," speech at an international conference on the future of NATO in Brussels on September 1, 1979, reprinted by *Survival*, November/December 1979.

The history of U.S. strategic targeting plans shows that urban-industrial targeting, the essence of assured destruction, is only a small fraction of the plans; counterforce targeting has always been emphasized. Ball points out that "even in the late 1960s, when Assured Destruction was stressed as the sole objective in U.S. declaratory policy, only about 11 percent of the targets in the National Strategic Target List (NSTL) were urban-industrial, and only about 10 percent of the SIOP weapons were allocated for delivery against urban-industrial targets."

Ball continues his argument by defending a U.S. emphasis on counter-force targeting and a transition toward the inclusion of strategic defense in a balanced policy of deterrence. In a compelling argument for the re-orientation of American nuclear doctrine along these two lines, Ball notes that, "notwithstanding the rhetoric of Assured Destruction as the guarantor of the nuclear peace, it would be irresponsible for U.S. policy-makers to deny themselves the capacity to limit damage to the United States in the event that nuclear war nevertheless occurs." He concludes his elucidation of the concept of deterrence with these words:

It follows, then, that strategic defences, at least in some configurations, are by no means necessarily incompatible with the declared U.S. basic strategic policy of deterrence. . . . strategic defences are simply another means—along with offensive strikes against Soviet nuclear capabilities and passive defences such as shelters and evacuation programs—of achieving deterrence. . . .[30]

I have intertwined threads of theology, intense emotional debate, partisan politics, and dispassionate doctrinal analysis in the foregoing para-graphs. I now return to the opening admission that the bitter attacks against strategic defense in the late 1960s were puzzling to me, and acknowledge that the great vindication of BMD, ushered in by the Pres-ident's announcement of SDI, has also brought excesses that are hard to comprehend. Some proponents of strategic defense have gone so far as to brand deterrence based on counterattack as "immoral." More subtly and insidiously, the opponents of strategic defense have resorted to denying that defense has any deterrent value, arguing indeed that it is a contradiction in terms, and that strategic defense must remain saddled with the burden of being inherently destabilizing. Many of these charges and countercharges have been cloaked in arcane jargon, and—what is worse—in loose and misleading shorthand labels. As Brzezinski, Jastrow, and Kampelman wrote,

our national debate over President Reagan's suggestion that the country develop a strategic defense against Soviet nuclear attack is taking on a theological dimension that has no

---

[30] Desmond Ball, "Strategic Defenses: Concepts and Programs," prepared for a conference on Strategic Defense and Soviet-American Relations, the Wilson Center, Smithsonian Institution, March 10-11, 1986.

place in a realistic search for a path out of the world's dilemma. . . . we must not abandon nuclear deterrence until we are convinced that a better means is at hand.[31]

Origins of the ABM Treaty: U.S. Rationale

Reference has already been made to the symbolic importance of the ABM Treaty to the arms control community despite the fact that it has been ineffective in achieving its original purpose. I would like to return to the Treaty in order to record some professional views about its origins, as well as my own observations about its implementation and the political fallout which it created in its first ten years. My point of view is that of one who worked in the trenches of BMD systems and technologies and as such did not examine the Treaty's objectives in the context of national policy. Because of this limitation, I am resolved to restrict my observations to the practical effects of the Treaty, rather than perform a comprehensive analysis of its doctrinal basis, of the negotiations that produced it, and of the subsequent record of compliance. This is no great loss to the literature, as there is a vast amount of such analytical and historical commentary readily available.

In order to establish a point of reference, I will confess that, while perplexed by the underlying theory, I was not instinctively opposed to limitations on ABM deployment. As previously noted, I joined the BMD program in the late 1960s, during the tempest of the national ABM debate, and soon became aware of the ongoing negotiations with the Soviet Union on both offensive and defensive systems. I recall with great clarity the ABM deployment decisions which formed a backdrop to the negotiations: Secretary McNamara's speech announcing the Sentinel decision in 1967 and President Nixon's announcement of the Safeguard decision in 1969. McNamara's speech was strange in that it was devoted almost entirely to why BMD is bad, but it wound up saying we would deploy a system to defend against the Chinese anyway. The Safeguard announcement was a carefully constructed shift in the mission of U.S. BMD, broadened to include defense against the Soviet Union and embellished with many checks and balances; however, it left the same system in place to perform a much different mission. In the following section, I will discuss further the mismatch of Safeguard components to the primary new mission of Minuteman defense, but for now let me observe only that its aging and non-optimum design features led many of us to feel that limiting its deployment would not be such a bad idea. This in no way disparages the technical excellence of Safeguard, given the vintage of its technology,

---

[31] Brzezinski, et al., op. cit., p. 28.

21

but simply acknowledges its vulnerability to shifting missions and advancing technology.

At some point around 1970, I was introduced to the thinking of the late Donald Brennan of the Hudson Institute. My first exposure to his views on strategic policy matters was from the *Congressional Record*, in testimony he had given before the House Foreign Affairs Committee. Having been depressed by the seemingly unanimous contempt that the "serious strategic thinkers" of the country had for BMD, I was encouraged by Brennan's pro-BMD views and the brilliance of his rationale for them. I can remember the exhilaration I felt on reading an authoritative statement of support for strategic defense, one which corroborated my own skepticism about a theory that branded BMD destabilizing, or even immoral, and vindicated my natural inclination to rank offensive weapons, particularly the emerging MIRV technology, as more destabilizing. Brennan provided an anchor to those of us who saw that the SALT I negotiations had become increasingly focused on the need for banning defense, and realized that the doctrinal justification of assured destruction was becoming more elaborate, extremist, puzzling, and dominant. Even for one such as myself, who could sympathize with the idea of limiting Safeguard deployment, the plausible reasons for doing so bore no resemblance to the bizarre theory which had gained ascendancy.

The most eloquent and cogent description of Brennan's ideas and his place in the history of strategic policy formulation has come from the physicist, Freeman Dyson. Writing in a memorable paper called "The Quest for Concept," Dyson captures Brennan's lonely efforts to bring sanity to the debate of the late 1960s, his vision of a better foundation for U.S. strategic policy that only now is gaining acceptance, and his relentless analytic rigor in advancing his views. Dyson refers to the same testimony of Donald Brennan that I cited above and notes that much of his testimony was opposed to MIRV. Going against the mainstream of professional thought, Brennan argued in vain that MIRV was more destabilizing than BMD and therefore should replace BMD at the top of the arms control agenda. In building his case, Brennan formulated a new concept which was presented in his testimony as follows:

Let us consider two principles. The first principle is that, in terms of strategic nuclear conflict, following any plausibly feasible Soviet attack, we should be able to do at least as badly unto the Soviets as they had done or could do unto us. The second principle is that we should prefer live Americans to dead Russians, whenever a choice between the two presents itself. The Soviets may be expected to prefer live Russians to dead Americans, and therein resides the basis for an important common interest; we may both prefer live

Americans and live Russians. This formulation may seem so simple as to sound facetious, and in a sense it is, but it conceals a point that is profoundly and surprisingly controversial.[32]

Thus, Brennan contrasted assured destruction, which he called the "Brass Rule," with a new formulation which Dyson labeled "Live and Let Live." His concept led to an unswerving belief in BMD and an unalterable opposition to any theory that portrayed BMD as intrinsically destabilizing. Of course, much of the philosophy imbedded in the above quotation is fully consistent with President Reagan's March 23, 1983 announcement of SDI, fourteen years later. Brennan would have reveled in the dramatic shift in strategic policy represented by SDI, and would have felt justifiable pride in his earlier identification with its basic tenets.

Origins of the ABM Treaty: Soviet Rationale

In his history of events leading up to the ABM treaty, Newhouse paints a meticulous portrait of the chief architect of assured destruction, Robert McNamara. In what has always seemed a watershed meeting between the superpowers, Newhouse recounts the Glassboro meeting between Johnson and Kosygin. He repeats the famous question by Kosygin, in response to Johnson's overture for banning ABM, about how could he tell the Russian people they could not defend themselves against U.S. rockets. (Kissinger's account says that "Kosygin in 1967 told President Johnson that the idea of not engaging in defense was one of the most ridiculous propositions that he had ever heard. . . .")[33] Reportedly, McNamara answered Kosygin's query with a "long, detailed and impassioned presentation" that seems to have started the long, tortuous trek toward the ABM Treaty. While there are some who believe that the Soviets were persuaded that banning defense was good for the same reasons McNamara proclaimed, I share Senator Moynihan's view that they never really accepted the assured destruction rationale for proscribing defense. Rather, the Soviets agreed to the ABM Treaty for the pragmatic reason that they feared the U.S. technological lead in this field and thought it prudent to freeze U.S. technology while they played catch-up.

Michael Deane records eight different reasons why the Soviets came to believe that BMD should be banned by treaty, none of which coincides with my view. He traces the change in Soviet attitude toward defense, starting from the incredulous response by Kosygin that anyone could ever consider banning defense to the final insistence by the Kremlin that

---

[32] Freeman J. Dyson, "The Quest for Concept," address before the Conference on the Arms Race, under the auspices of the Princeton Episcopalian and Presbyterian Churches, September 27-28, 1980.

[33] Kissinger, op. cit,. p. 267.

BMD be banned in the latter stages of the SALT I process. To explain this flip-flop in the Soviet position, he infers that the Soviets came to believe that the cost of BMD was too high, that the money might be better used for domestic and civilian needs, that BMD was ineffective, that it would exacerbate the arms race; and he cites other similar straightforward reasons. He seems to shun the conclusion that they deliberately set out to sidetrack U.S. BMD efforts. However, he recognizes that the Soviet Union has made important strides in strategic defense since the Treaty, in combination with their massive buildup in strategic offensive weapons, and he warns, in dire terms:

This asymmetry if permitted to endure virtually guarantees that in case of a nuclear war the United States will suffer defeat and probably annihilation as a functioning society while the USSR and its system will survive, and with sufficient power intact, to establish the world hegemony that its leadership has always considered its ultimate due. . . .[34]

Sid Graybeal and Daniel Goure subscribe to the theory that the Soviets agreed to the treaty in order to arrest U.S. technology in strategic defense.

Soviet sensitivity to new technologies has been particularly apparent in the area of BMD. Despite some of Moscow's statements to the contrary, it is readily apparent that during the SALT I negotiations the Soviet Union had little confidence in the viability of its ABM technology and had granted to the United States a definite lead in this field. The deployment of a workable U.S. ABM coupled with the American advantage in MIRV technology presented the Soviet Union with a rather bleak picture of the near future. The Soviets could not but expect the United States to use this military-technological advantage to reverse Soviet political gains. To forestall such a disadvantageous situation and to close the technological gap between the two countries, the Soviet Union sought in its arms control strategy to limit U.S. ABM programs, perhaps with the additional hope that deployment limitations might adversely affect the U.S. R&D program.[35]

If indeed the Soviets anticipated that the United States would overreact and curtail allowable BMD R&D as well as comply with the limitations on deployment, they could not have been closer to the mark. For about one decade the U.S. BMD program was severely constrained by the U.S. Congress while the Soviet program proceeded unabated.

Leon Sloss is even more blunt about the Soviet leaders' reasons for agreeing to the ABM Treaty.

The Treaty was successfully negotiated because the United States had a program that the Soviets wanted to stop. In the early 1970s, Moscow reached the conclusion that U.S. antimissile technology was substantially advanced beyond that of the Soviet Union. Thus,

---

[34] Michael J. Deane, *The Role of Strategic Defense in Soviet Strategy* (Miami, Florida: Advanced International Studies Institute, in association with the University of Miami, July 1980).

[35] Harvard University, *U.S. Arms Control Objectives and the Implications for Ballistic Missile Defense*, proceedings of a symposium held at the Center for Science and International Affairs, November 1-2, 1979.

the Soviets sought to buy time to catch up. . . . the Soviets are motivated primarily by direct considerations of self-interest, rather than by concepts of 'stability.'[36]

Another expression that Brennan coined was that the Interim Offensive Agreement, signed at the same time as the ABM Treaty, did the "right thing poorly" and the ABM Treaty did the "wrong thing well." As a matter of historical record, it would be hard to argue with this judgment. Even though there was widespread sentiment, reinforced by the Jackson Amendment to the Senate ratification bill, that the ABM Treaty was subject to termination if subsequent accords were not reached on offensive arms, the Soviets could not have been more blatant in their disregard for this linkage in arms control. They continued to build one generation ICBM system after another, as well as other strategic weapons, thereby magnifying the most destabilizing element in the strategic equation. They concentrated on the accurate, land-based MIRV systems that Brennan properly identified as the real danger to strategic stability. They succeeded in trumping our ace card through the ABM Treaty, which simultaneously froze BMD deployment and, what was worse, created a euphoric mood in the U.S. Congress that militated against appropriating funds for permissible BMD research and development.

U.S. Compliance with the ABM Treaty

In the period immediately following the signing of the ABM Treaty, there was a massive effort within the BMD organization to inventory every shred of BMD activity to assure compliance with the terms and conditions of the Treaty. From that time on, the U.S. record of compliance was one of total, scrupulous, "beyond a shadow of a doubt" observance of even the most vague prohibitions of the Treaty. It was often a case of "bending over backward" not only to comply with the letter of the Treaty, but also to avoid appearances that could lead to misinterpretation. Following the signing of the protocol agreement in 1974, reducing the number of allowed sites from two to one, the Malmstrom site, which we already had under construction, was subjected to one of the most elaborate processes of demolition in the history of military construction. Every "re-bar" was meticulously extracted, heavy structures were totally flattened, and all cavities were ceremoniously filled with concrete in order to leave no doubt that the site had been obliterated. This was typical of the extreme precaution taken to comply totally with the Treaty.

Of course, the ABM Treaty was, and is, primarily a treaty limiting deployment quantities—one site, 100 interceptors, 100 launchers, and 18 radars (plus two large radars)—not a restriction on research and development.

---

[36] Leon Sloss, "The Return of Strategic Defense," *Strategic Review*, Summer 1984.

However, some of the articles of the Treaty, and agreed statements accompanying the Treaty, impinge on BMD R&D. For example, Article V stipulates that each party undertakes not to "develop, test, or deploy ABM systems or components which are sea-based, air-based, space-based, or mobile land-based." Gerard Smith, the chief U.S. negotiator of the ABM Treaty, has testified to the Senate Armed Services Committee that what is meant by "develop and test" is that phase following laboratory development when field testing is initiated on a prototype or "breadboard" model. Of course, this definition is practically enforced by the inability to monitor or detect, by national technical means, any development activity prior to this phase. However, the force of this "mobility" exclusion has come under considerable scrutiny and debate with the advent of the SDI emphasis on space basing: Can space-based SDI components be tested in space to determine if they work? It is too early to have a showdown on this issue, but it will surely continue to cloud the SDI thrust toward space basing.

A less provocative case of mobile BMD components was raised by the LoAD/Sentry system several years ago, when that system was being considered for basing with various mobile (deceptive) basing modes of MX. In keeping with the extreme measures to assure compliance, described above, the plan was to bolt down the LoAD/Sentry components during tests at the national ranges (this plan was not implemented because the program was canceled in 1984). It is not at all clear that the Soviets were equally scrupulous in testing their ABM-X-3 system, which is also a mobile system.

An interesting exclusion is embodied in Agreed Statement "E" of the Treaty attachments. This provision prohibits multiple-kill vehicles on the same interceptor. I have been told on good authority that this provision was initiated by the U.S. delegation, based on its knowledge of the U.S. HIT (homing interceptor technology) program. HIT was a program carried out to demonstrate that a miniature "hit-to-kill" vehicle could be developed that would allow multiple vehicles to be carried on a single interceptor, each with nonnuclear lethality against an offensive nuclear warhead. (This program, successfully demonstrated by the Army in laboratory tests, evolved into the current U.S. ASAT program.) The concept was attractive at the time of negotiations and for some years thereafter because of the leverage it afforded the defense. In a sense, the concept was one of fighting MIRV with MIRV. (Although it is no longer fashionable, it was a good idea.) Reportedly, the Soviets did not know what the U.S. delegation was talking about when it was proposed that this technology be banned, but a patient explanation (reminiscent of McNamara's explanation of assured destruction to Kosygin) "won them over to agreement."

Those of us who were fond of the concept were distressed about this classic case of the United States shooting itself in the foot.

Political Fallout of the ABM Treaty

The period following the signing of the ABM Treaty was a melancholy one for those of us who were trying to maintain funding for BMD research and development. The U.S. Congress overreacted to the Treaty and continually slashed the budget requests for allowed research and development. The Congress was understandably euphoric that a bona fide treaty limiting strategic systems had been signed with the Soviet Union, but it was shortsighted about the need for remaining up to date in defensive technology and the consequences of giving the Soviets an advantage in the pace of technological exploration. The environment in the hearing rooms of the Armed Services and Appropriations Committees in both Houses of Congress became extremely hostile toward ballistic missile defense. This was especially true of that part of the BMD program and budget having to do with systems development. During this period, the BMD budget was about equally divided between systems and advanced technology development, and the flak attracted by the former exceeded that by the latter by orders of magnitude. In a somewhat rueful joke, we used to say that we must, at all costs, avoid showing any systems relevance of the technology we were pursuing.

In Fiscal Year (FY) 1974, the Congress took a massive bite out of the advanced technology part of the BMD budget request. This was a complete reversal of form and reveals much about the mood on the Hill at this time toward BMD. The explanation for this action, amounting to a budget cut of $42.4 million from a total advanced technology budget request of about $100 million, was that the technology was associated with light area defense. Senator Symington was the floor manager of the Senate Authorization Bill that inflicted this cut, and he singled out this action proudly in introducing the bill on the floor. He observed that the light area defense program was a good example of the "deviousness," or some such word, of the Pentagon in trying to slip through a treaty-prohibited BMD program. Actually, the program was nothing of the sort: It was purely advanced technology, emphasizing what was at that time the very embryonic field of long-wave infrared optics—of the type that led to the successful Homing Overlay Experiment eleven years later.

It must be said that the Administration was not too wise to package BMD technology in the wrappings of a provocative BMD mission, light area defense. Congressional opposition to different BMD missions exhibited varying degrees of intensity, according to the "stability rules" of assured

27

destruction. City defense was much more evil than silo defense (defense of Minuteman sites, or silos). Despite the reasoned plea of Herman Kahn four years earlier for "thin defense" (another name for light area defense), and the official acceptance of this defense mission during the Sentinel deployment period, it fell from grace precipitously after the ABM Treaty.[37] But it will never be known whether it was the Administration's tactical mistake of inviting the charge of guilt by association or the Senate's seizure of an opportunity to "stick it to BMD" that led to this cut of perfectly harmless, allowable, and critical technology.

In an attempt to get the FY74 BMD advanced technology budget cut restored, I made a valiant (if maladroit) maneuver to transmit a white paper through the Pentagon to the relevant Congressional committees. Then-Secretary of the Army Callaway was in Huntsville shortly after the axe fell on BMD, and I gave his military aide a copy of an eighteen-page paper I had written, explaining the virtues of the technology which had been eliminated and the seriousness of the error the Senate had made in misinterpreting this technology. I cautioned the aide to protect my anonymity; he assured me he would. The next day I received an irate phone call from my boss in Washington, inquiring about the "Bill Davis" white paper. To my dismay the white paper, although appreciated by Secretary Callaway, did not result in restoration of the budget. It did succeed in getting me into some hot water. It was a bitter lesson learned about the workings of the Hill, perhaps most pointedly of the fact that once a ploy is set in motion, or alternatively, once a mistake is made, there is no turning it around.

About four years later, in fiscal year 1978, I inherited the job of principal liaison with Congressional staffers and civilian deputy to the BMD Program Manager, in shepherding the BMD budget through the annual Congressional cycle. During this period, the BMD Program Manager, a one- or two-star Army general officer, reported to the Vice Chief of Staff of the Army and testified directly to the various committees of Congress on the program. As the civilian deputy to the Program Manager, I represented continuity and technical backup in this process. Over a period of six fiscal years, during which three different generals served as program manager, I participated in the Congressional cycles. It was an experience that revealed much about the complexity of the committee process on the Hill, the ministrations of the Pentagon, the nature of the "Iron Triangle" of Hill-Pentagon-Industry, and, especially, the precarious existence of a controversial, treaty-limited defense program.

---

[37] Herman Kahn, "The Case for a Thin System," Hudson Institute Paper HI-1185/3-P, May 27, 1969.

During the mid-1970s, as previously noted, the only form of BMD R&D that was tolerated in the Congress and, hence, in the Pentagon, was that clearly associated with advanced technology. An overwhelming majority of members and staffers on the Hill believed either that advanced technology was the only permissible R&D activity or that it was the only program that could get passed. Systems work was anathema. It was only through the most heroic efforts that a few players from the Defense Department, Congressional staffs, and industry managed to preserve some vestige of systems work in this period—and only then through disguise, persistence, and byzantine negotiations.

The intensity of the campaign to structure the BMD program in a saleable, long-range research package, in response to the Congressional mood, led to some rather bizarre programming activities at the working level of the BMD organization. There was a contest among middle managers to see who could reach furthest out into the realm of exotic and high risk technology to gain approval of their programs. The overriding guidance was "do not be pedestrian in defining your program." Hence, the Advanced Technology Program (ATP) took on the appearance of a DARPA program, or perhaps a collection of research tasks more resembling those undertaken by the National Science Foundation. Hardly any industry proposal became too weird or far-fetched to gain favorable consideration for BMD funding. The center-of-gravity of BMD became skewed toward very long-range pursuits that were guaranteed not to threaten the "spirit" of the Treaty or antagonize the most liberal Senator.

In the late 1970s, the prevailing Congressional attitude toward BMD began to shift; more and more questions were raised about "when can you deploy a system?" Deployment leadtimes again became a concern. Interest in building systems prototypes crept back into the picture. To illustrate the completeness of the reversal, a Congressional prohibition against prototyping BMD systems, passed in the mid-1970s era of anti-systems sentiment, was reversed in FY79; the new language encouraged the Defense Department to get on with prototyping. William Schneider, then serving as a staffer to Representative Kemp on the Defense Subcommittee of the House Appropriations Committee, was instrumental in getting this prohibition removed.

It is not possible to trace all of the reasons for this shift in Congressional sentiment toward BMD, but it is a good bet that Soviet strides in developing BMD systems had a lot to do with it. The Soviets never slackened the pace of their BMD systems development work following the Treaty. They had no apparent misgivings about violating the "spirit" of the Treaty. They relentlessly pursued prototype system development, for one generation after another, while continuously upgrading their technical prowess in BMD and reducing leadtimes to a potential deployment. As contrasted with the blatant case of Krasnoyarsk, the Soviets appeared to stay within the bounds of the treaty in the seventies. They worked, however, right up to the edge.

The revival of interest in deployment leadtimes was most pronounced in the House Armed Services Committee (HASC). In FY78 Anthony Battista, the prominent HASC staffer, championed the development and deployment leadtimes for all classes of weapons systems as a *cause célèbre*. He deplored the stretched-out weapons acquisition process that had evolved in the Defense Department, and used every example and illustration he could get his hands on to dramatize the problem. In one discussion I had with Battista during this period, he mentioned an impressive "gimmick" used by John McDaniel, technical director of the Missile Command laboratories, which was reported in the *Armed Forces Journal*. The gimmick was a large scroll which rolled out impressively to reveal the extraordinarily long time period and large number of review decisions required to get a weapon system through the formal acquisition process. In a moment of questionable discretion on my part, I agreed to hand-carry the scroll to Battista on my next trip to Washington. I borrowed the scroll from John McDaniel, my former boss and mentor, and took it to Washington. It proved to be quite a physical undertaking since it was about the size of a BMD interceptor, but it satisfied Battista's purposes only too well. He displayed it to the full HASC—all thirty feet of milestones. It was a smash hit. Congressman Ichord was still talking about it weeks later when I accompanied the BMD Program Manager to testify before Ichord's R&D subcommittee.

The irony of the marked transition from an emphasis on pure research to insistence on short deployment leadtimes, perhaps too obvious to state, is that the Congress and the compliant leaders in the Pentagon professed no awareness of the guidance that got us into a stretched-out posture—which they, of course, had created. It was futile to complain that leadtimes had been stretched out because of the widespread antipathy toward BMD systems development, even to the point of prohibiting prototype development. Fortunately, the bureaucratic inertia within the BMD community, which Henry Kissinger once poignantly decried as a general government curse, prevented the total disappearance of systems effort and preserved some semblance of a systems framework.

The resurgence of interest in BMD leadtimes was not as great on the Senate side as on the House side. Larry Smith, lead staffer in the Senate Armed Services Committee (SASC) during the Democratic majority era of the late 1970s, was a student of BMD but not an advocate of accelerated development to reduce leadtimes. To his great credit, he acted vigorously to insert language into the SASC authorization bill, in 1978 or 1979, to stabilize the BMD budget at a constant level of effort (prior year budget plus inflation). This was a landmark event. Budget cuts and restrictive Congressional language had so violently wracked the program from year to year that it was not possible to plan or execute a coherent program. Viewed in retrospect, however, it is difficult to assess the net effect of SASC actions toward the BMD program. It was always clear that Senator McIntyre, chairman of the R&D subcommittee, viewed BMD with a great deal of suspicion. His writings and statements left no doubt that he was a true believer in the theory of assured destruction, and this was reflected in his dual attacks on strategic defense and improved ballistic missile accuracy. This latter position, opposition to accuracy, ranks second only to opposition to defense in its defiance of common sense. It can be traced to the fear of gaining a counterforce capability, anathema to all adherents of assured destruction.

Strategic Defense Conferences: Building an Intellectual Consensus

Concurrently with the Congressional shift back toward an interest in BMD systems and deployment leadtimes in the late 1970s, a series of conferences were held for the purpose of examining emerging trends in the strategic-military relationships between the United States and the Soviet Union with specific emphasis on the implications for BMD. The BMD Advanced Technology Center in Huntsville was the sponsoring agency for these conferences under the leadership of Wallace Kirkpatrick. Kirkpatrick, author of a recently published award-winning paper on strategic defense,[38] collaborated with Robert L. Pfaltzgraff, Jr., and Jacquelyn Davis, of the Institute for Foreign Policy Analysis (IFPA), in formulating a plan for these conferences in which the generally positive technical doctrinal and political aspects of BMD would be aired. They correctly perceived that a growing number of strategic thinkers on campuses, in think tanks, in the government, and in industry would be receptive to forums in which objective support for strategic defense would be tolerated and even encouraged. Although dissenting views on BMD were included in these conferences, their main thrust was to counterbalance the widespread academic antagonism toward BMD. Over the period from 1977 through 1980, eleven such conferences were held by the Institute for Foreign Policy Analysis, Harvard University, and the University of Ala-

---

[38] Wallace E. Kirkpatrick, "Emerging Strategic Environment: Implications for Strategic Defense," *Defense Science 2001 +*, August 1983.

bama in Huntsville. Most of these conferences were arranged by IFPA in Washington, D.C.

It is not possible to assess confidently, even with the advantage of six years' hindsight, how influential these conferences were in crystallizing informed opinion on BMD. However, it seems likely that they had a great deal of spin-off effect, if for no other reason than the stature and influence of the individual participants. As the series progressed, the conferences attracted increasing numbers of high-level participants from all segments of the strategic community. It almost seemed that there was pent-up demand for a forum in which it was respectable to express support for strategic defense. While the intellectual force of the conferences came principally from IFPA, the Hudson Institute, the Advanced International Studies Institute associated with the University of Miami, and similar centers of strategic thought, the meetings profited greatly from the views of representatives from the Hill, the Pentagon, industry, and other government agencies. Significantly, our European allies also displayed a great deal of interest in these meetings and they regularly participated. The sessions at these conferences were marked by a strong sense of impending change in strategic policy and programs.

Strategic Defense Revival in the Reagan Era

With the inauguration of President Reagan, the fortunes of BMD soared. Large increases in the BMD budget were requested by the Administration, and interest in BMD systems became greater than interest in pure technology. Although it did not fare as well as the President's Strategic Modernization Program, the BMD program enjoyed some of the benefits of the President's magic in getting defense spending increases through the Congress. The LoAD system, the generation under development at the time of the 1980 election, was boosted from a low level investigation to a program involving hundreds of millions of dollars. As always, however, there were problems along with the higher visibility and appropriations. There was a vocal minority among the new Administration's advisers who fought LoAD on the grounds that it was too complex, or that it could not be deceptively based with MX. The most vexing problem was the return of the contingent arguing in support of "simple, novel, low-cost, rapidly deployable" systems—which I called "junk" systems by this time. Encouraged by the Administration's interest in a "quick-fix" for strategic weapons deficiencies,[39] a host of amateur BMD designers rushed their ideas into

---

[39] William R. Van Cleave and W. Scott Thompson, *Strategic Options for the Early Eighties: What Can Be Done?* (White Plains, Md.: Automated Graphic Systems, Inc., 1979).

print. All of the ideas promised lower cost and shorter leadtimes than LoAD.

In an historical peak for the "junk" class of BMD systems, a concept began circulating in the Pentagon that was either a hoax or the most damning indictment of past BMD over-design and gold-plating sins that could possibly be advanced. It consisted of a conglomeration of existing air defense radars and hybrid interceptors, and claimed to be capable of outperforming any traditional system at a tiny fraction of the cost. It did not require any appreciable R&D; it was virtually impervious to penetration by attacking ICBM warheads (it was accompanied by the only flat draw-down curve—i.e., Minuteman survivors versus arriving warheads—I have ever seen); it was nuclear hard, reliable, and insensitive to penetration aids; and its investment cost was nil. The remarkable thing was that the system received such serious attention. It was brought to Secretary Weinberger's attention, and the Army BMD organization was asked to evaluate it. It was difficult to evaluate a concept that was so totally devoid of merit, but a solemn recitation of its myriad weaknesses was duly sent to the Pentagon. Nothing was ever heard about this concept thereafter. It is interesting to reflect on how violently the fads and fashions of strategic defense systems can swing in a few years. The system just described was seriously considered during the same Administration that began SDI, the opposite pole in complexity and sophistication.

Another anomaly in strategic defense approaches in the early transition period of the Reagan Administration was an intensive effort by a small group of evangelists to deploy a space-based laser system in the near term. The system was proposed by an industry group which gained the appellation of the "gang of four" (not the same gang as previously described). Again, the group stirred up an amazing amount of interest and garnered a level of support that was all out of proportion to the quality of their proposal (basically, they advocated deployment of a constellation of 5/4 chemical lasers—5 megawatts of power and 4 meter mirrors). The U.S. Senate, in particular, was attracted to the promises of a system that could be deployed in the 1980s and could annihilate the Soviet large ICBMs and their manned bombers should they attempt an attack. A significant number of Senators voted for this space-based system in its various incarnations over the period of the early 1980s.

In a speech to the AIAA strategic systems symposium in 1980, I challenged the realism of some of the claims of the advocates of this early space-based system and called attention to its harm in siphoning off support from mainstream BMD programs. I was roundly criticized by some of the concept's more influential backers, but eventually the con-

33

spicuous flaws in the concept, now amplified by the long-term planning horizon for such systems under SDI, led to its undoing. It is considered axiomatic in SDI today that an effective space-based laser weapon system requires power levels and mirror diameters (translatable to the figure-of-merit of brightness) orders of magnitude greater than proposed by the industrial gang of four.

With the President's dramatic announcement of SDI in March 1983, BMD moved to center stage of the national agenda as it never had before. During the Sentinel and Safeguard eras, two different Administrations recommended BMD deployments; but the prestige and influence of the White House had never been employed as forcefully as in President Reagan's advocacy of SDI. It was never clear, in the case of President Johnson's and President Nixon's association with BMD, that they had their hearts in their deployment decisions. It is clear that President Reagan believes fervently in SDI. Moreover, the channels for argument within the Administration have narrowed and stabilized from the violent lurching and weaving brought on by the extremely primitive and unrealistically exotic systems that cropped up on an almost daily basis. As noted above, there has been confusion in statements about what SDI is, but the range of technical approaches being considered has narrowed tremendously.

In assessing the chances of gaining long-term support for SDI in the Congress, one has to wonder if subsequent Administrations, whether Republican or Democratic, can capture the imagination for strategic defense as President Reagan has done. He has somehow elevated the subject from a struggle over dollars to a lofty debate over breaking away from the threat of retaliation and embracing the idea of protecting lives from nuclear holocaust. It almost seems that the opposition is intimidated by the sheer virtue of this position.

Another significant difference in the current debate over SDI and the ABM debate of the late 1960s is that today the target is much more nebulous. In the debate of the late 1960s there was a well-defined BMD system, Safeguard, to attack. Garwin, Bethe, Rathjens and others could point with precision to the weaknesses of the system: it was vulnerable to attack, it could be blacked out by nuclear fireballs, it could be spoofed by penetration aids. It is more difficult to attack SDI because it is a research program with no well-defined system. Poke a hole in this concept, we will change the concept; if you do not like this technology, we will show you two dozen others. It is an amorphous mass of research on many parallel tracks.

Perhaps this same "researchy" nature will prove a disadvantage to SDI over the long haul. How long will the Congress be sympathetic to a multibillion dollar per year research program? How long can interest be sustained in an open-ended technology program with little or no convergence toward a realizable weapon system? I used to think that similar research programs, such as the BMD Advanced Technology Program, the Advanced Ballistic Reentry Systems program, and the Defense Advanced Research Project Agency program had a certain budget ceiling, above which the Congress would not provide support over a long period of years. Although this ceiling was never precise, it appeared that the tolerance of Congress for this kind of program was in the vicinity of several hundred million dollars per year. If there is any merit in this theory, the multibillion dollar level of SDI will encounter Congressional impatience after a few years and increasing insistence on some visible product other than research results.

Soviet Post-Treaty BMD Development: Doctrine and Hardware

In attempting to understand the direction of Soviet strategic force developments in the post-Treaty period, it is important to analyze what doctrine, political framework, and motivations shape and channel their programs. Obviously, they are embarked in a fundamentally different direction than the United States. That marked difference in direction is explained by different experts on the Soviet Union in vastly different ways. I have chosen the Garthoff-Pipes debate as representative of the poles of opinion.

Raymond Garthoff acknowledges that "Soviet acceptance of sharply constrained BMD was certainly facilitated by the fact that the United States had a much superior BMD defense technology and thus capabilities for an important lead in BMD deployment in the 1970s," but he also contends that the Soviet Union had a serious interest in arms control, detente, and the concept of mutual deterrence. This latter view, Soviet acceptance of mutual deterrence, stands in sharp contrast to Senator Moynihan's conclusion, quoted earlier, and a large body of opinion by other students of Soviet nuclear strategy. Garthoff first elaborated his thesis that there is basic agreement in Soviet and U.S. strategic doctrine in a lengthy article in *International Security* in 1978. This article was reprinted in abridged form in *Strategic Review* in 1982, along with a rebuttal by Richard Pipes.[40]

Pipes takes issue with Garthoff's argument that there exists a fundamental identity of view as well as interests between the United States and the Soviet Union concerning the nature and use of strategic nuclear weapons. He then observes that in order to adduce a convincing case about Soviet strategic doctrine and intentions, one must draw on data regarding actual

---

[40] Raymond L. Garthoff, "Mutual Deterrence and Strategic Arms Limitation in Soviet Policy," and Richard Pipes, "Soviet Strategic Doctrine: Another View," *Strategic Review*, Fall 1982.

Soviet strategic programs and deployments, as well as Soviet writings. He criticizes Garthoff for entirely ignoring the evidence relating to Soviet hardware, in preference for what he charges are highly selective quotations from Soviet literature. (As shown in Chapter 1, the current policy of the United States regarding strategic defense can be portrayed in any way desired by selective quotation.) In what seems to be the most telling refutation of the Garthoff position, Pipes has this to say:

> If Ambassador Garthoff's view is to prevail, he must explain the reasons for the steady Soviet emphasis on heavy, land-based ballistic missiles, culminating in the decision taken in the 1960s to proceed with the production of the SS-18 and SS-19, two major counterforce systems of great throwweight and high accuracies with MIRV payloads two to three times those of Minuteman III. He would further need to explain the attention lavished in the USSR on strategic defenses, including air defense and civil defense programs that do not fit mutual deterrence doctrines and have no adequate counterparts in the United States.[41]

Perhaps it is natural for one who has been involved in the engineering and technology side of strategic systems, and who has no illusions about having expertise in strategic theory, to be attracted to Pipes' logic that the nature of the weapons you are building is a more reliable guide to your intentions than what you say. As Jastrow explained so clearly in the quotation in Chapter 1, there can be no doubt about what the large Soviet ICBM force was designed and deployed for. I have asked many knowledgeable people over the years if there was an alternative hypothesis to the obvious one that it is for a counterforce capability against our deterrent forces. No one has ever given me a plausible alternative. Therefore, it stretches the imagination beyond limit to believe that the Soviets share our deep-rooted faith in assured destruction (or "mutual deterrence" as Garthoff and Pipes put it). As the Soviets continue to upgrade their large ICBM force, they mock any apologist who contends that they are merely seeking a minimal deterrent force.

The objectives of the Soviet BMD program over the past twenty years have been more difficult to interpret than their massive ICBM buildup. Many anomalies in the direction of their BMD developments have puzzled intelligence analysts and the U.S. BMD community alike. Why were they so late in going to a hot terminal interceptor (Sprintski)? Why have they persisted in using radar frequencies that are susceptible to nuclear blackout? What is the reason for their enchantment with dish radars for missile tracking? It is easy to dismiss these questions with the smug response that they are simply technologically inferior to U.S. BMD designers. However, aside from its arrogance, this response fails the test required by functional and utility analyses of their BMD systems—which invariably reveal that, given certain modest defense objectives, their systems per-

---

[41] Pipes, op. cit.

form admirably against our strategic ballistic missiles. This seems to be a universal truth regarding Soviet weapon systems: they often appear to be crude by U.S. standards, but they work.

A pregnant phrase in the preceding paragraph was "given certain modest defense objectives." In order to make any sense at all out of Soviet BMD activities, this proviso must be understood. Particularly now, with the SDI focus on the development of a virtually perfect BMD, it is difficult to adjust one's thinking to defense objectives that are far more modest. But, taking the Moscow BMD system as an example, the Soviets have nurtured and preserved this seemingly primitive and flawed system for a period of thirty years. Now, with its recent upgrades, it represents a respectable, two-layer system very similar to the one recommended in Chapter 1 as a responsive hedge option for the U.S. program. What has been its defense objective? Many have laughingly pointed to the host of ways it could be penetrated by sophisticated U.S. offensive systems. (It is noteworthy, however, that the U.S. Strategic Air Command has never laughed.) But, if one thinks of lesser objectives than blunting a concerted U.S. first strike, an extremely unlikely scenario in the first place, then it makes a great deal of sense. Obviously, it has great utility in protecting against an "Nth country" attack, such as from China, but it also has value in defending against a U.S. retaliatory attack.

I remember the first time, in the mid-1970s, when I realized that the whole Soviet BMD program, unlike our own, was designed to work in concert with their ICBM first-strike counterforce capability. My "Eureka" reaction seems out of place now, since this scenario is so widely understood and accepted. However, ten years ago the revelation came from an obscure study performed in the BMD Advanced Technology Center in Huntsville. Its findings cleared up many mysteries that had perplexed me about what the Soviets were up to. To be sure, their Moscow system and their ABM-X-3 rapidly deployable system were crude by our standards, but they would work fine against a thin, ragged U.S. retaliatory strike composed mostly of SLBMs. Under the rubric of a unifying doctrine of damage limitation, a separate "religion" from assured destruction, they could strike first to knock out our ICBM force and then defend against our retaliatory forces. They could even defend cities.

It almost seemed unfair that the threat we had to respond to in U.S. BMD studies consisted of thousands of warheads raining down on our ICBM fields and other military targets, while planners in the Soviet Union only had to cope with a thin retaliatory strike, spread over a large number of Soviet targets. It could get by with a more modest defense system because it had a more modest threat to counter. This asymmetry in both doctrine and force structure is so fundamental to an understanding of U.S.-Soviet strategic defense programs that it cannot be over-emphasized.

In a remarkable display of harmony, Secretary of Defense Weinberger and Secretary of State Shultz both signed a Preface to a special report in *National Defense* entitled "Soviet Strategic Defense Programs." This preface gives official weight to the Soviet defense objectives discussed above:

A summary of key Soviet offensive force developments is presented in the annex to this document, since those are critical to an understanding of the impact of Soviet strategic defense programs. Soviet offensive forces are designed to be able to limit severely U.S. and allied capability to retaliate against attack. Soviet defensive systems in turn are designed to prevent those retaliatory forces which did survive an attack from destroying Soviet targets.[42]

The prima facie evidence of Soviet intentions in strategic defense, then, is cut from the same fabric as their large buildup in ICBMs: a dedication to the doctrine of damage limitation and a rejection of assured destruction. While Garthoff presents a well-documented case for the reverse conclusion from Soviet writings, their strategic weapons investment strategy belies the declarations of some Soviet spokesmen. As the succeeding fourteen years of intensive effort to achieve a counterforce capability and an ABM breakout potential have proved, the Kremlin's assent to the ABM Treaty did not denote acceptance of assured destruction.

The Prudent U.S. Response:
A Rapidly Deployable BMD Hedge Option

What then do we do to checkmate the menacing posture the Soviets have assumed through their long, unswerving commitment to damage limitation? Can we "mirror image" their forces and restore the balance? Not likely. The President's Strategic Modernization Program will go far toward closing the gap, but at the end of this program we will be left with a marked inferiority in the wherewithal to inflict a counterforce strike. The SDI program could provide the remedy—if it incorporated a near-term element, as proposed in Chapter 1. It could be tailored to blunt a counterforce strike, or at least introduce enough uncertainty to act as a deterrent. However, the problem is time urgent: The Soviets have the forces in place, or within months of deployment, to back up their doctrine. We cannot safely rely on a strategic defense program that has a planning horizon of decades rather than years.

---

[42] "Soviet Strategic Defense Programs," *National Defense*, Special Supplement, November 1985.

In Chapter 1, I quoted a *Wall Street Journal* editorial entitled "Winnable Nuclear War," which made the startling allegation, citing NIE 11-3-885 as a source, that the Soviets have begun mass production of their ABM-X-3 system. The broader context of that editorial was that the Soviets are building a wide range of strategic weapons at a pace that increases their margin of strategic superiority every year and poses an extremely serious, near-term threat to the United States. The editorial describes a "furious Soviet warhead expansion, from 6,000 in 1978 to perhaps 12,000 today and 20,000 by 1990." It notes that their total production of offensive nuclear warheads in 1984 exceeded that of the United States by a ratio of greater than two to one. Their progress in ASW, "stealth technology," and other areas of strategic technology presents, in the aggregate, a chilling picture of both enormous stockpiles of weapons and improving quality and sophistication of weapons.

But it is the prescription for U.S. action advocated by the *Wall Street Journal* that I want to emphasize. I believe that it is a profoundly correct course of action (with the caveat that it be restricted to R&D preparation at this time, as described below) both because it plays to our strength and because it is the best of a dwindling number of plausible options. The following excerpts are pertinent:

As the U.S. adheres to MAD, trying to match the Soviets offense-for-offense, it will likely fall further behind. Aside from the obvious short-term limits on weapons-production capacity, there may be political limits on how long a democracy can compete in such a demoralizing race . . . .

Thus the U.S. needs not a few hundred more warheads but a dramatic increase in the security of 8,000 existing warheads. The answer: Defend those forces. Mr. Reagan already proposes a shield to render nuclear weapons obsolete. Early layers, based on the ground, could be started now. This would be a step away from MAD and toward a multilayer shield for cities. It may be the only way to meet the threat to deterrence itself.[43]

One of the vexing things in thinking about the strategic balance is that there are a seemingly endless series of moves and countermoves which can be postulated. Some analysts, including some of my good friends in the BMD community, observe that if we deploy a BMD system to defend our deterrent forces, the Soviets will do the same and, hence, raise the ante for our retaliatory strike requirements (technically, the Soviets may defend somewhat different assets than the United States, but the argument remains the same). They argue that in a world where both the United States and the Soviet Union have equal defenses, and the USSR retains a marked advantage in offensive forces, the United States would fare worse from an exchange than if neither side had defenses. I do not doubt

---

[43] *Wall Street Journal,* op. cit.

the accuracy of this observation from a force exchange point of view, but it begs the questions of reinstating deterrence, and of the relative security of this state of affairs versus one in which only the Soviets have a strategic defense.

What is the fable? The fox knows many things, but the hedgehog knows only one thing. I know only that if the Soviets break out from the ABM Treaty, or "creep out" as some observers think more likely, we will be confronted with a highly unstable situation in which the ability to respond promptly with a BMD deployment of our own would be required. True, an ensuing nuclear exchange may leave us at a disadvantage, but such an exchange would be less likely to occur if we have our forces defended. I am talking about a response option, not a unilateral decision to deploy a BMD system. I am not convinced at this point that it would be in our best interest to initiate a breakout in order to defend our deterrent forces, as implied by the *Wall Street Journal* editorial. However, I am persuaded that an intensive R&D effort to prepare for a rapid deployment, in response to a breakout on their part, would be prudent. In fact, the price of not doing so is frightening to contemplate.

Leon Sloss quotes James A. Thompson, of the Rand Corporation, in making a point about the difference in the stakes between the United States and the Soviet Union in strategic defense. It is a point which desperately needs to be understood in the current debate. I will attempt to establish the background and reasons for this difference in the next chapter, but for now it should be before us as a warning:

. . . were we able to obtain a significant advantage over the USSR in strategic defenses, we could have a substantial measure of strategic superiority over them. This would be to our advantage. By the same token, however, should the Soviets obtain a significant advantage over us, the results could be strategically catastrophic for the United States.[44]

---

[44] Sloss, op. cit., p. 43.

3. BMD Missions, Systems, and Technology

Definition and Interdependence of the Three BMD Factors

This chapter will not be a formal "BMD 101" tutorial. Instead, its purpose is to fill in some gaps that show up in the current literature, trace some threads of experience with BMD systems and technology, draw some contrasts between U.S. and Soviet BMD development, expose a number of myths that cloud the current debate, stress a few principles that have emerged from past BMD development, and justify a shift in emphasis in the SDI program along the lines suggested in the previous two chapters. With respect to the latter point—a shift toward more near-term emphasis—I will continue to pursue this central theme within the context of a balanced SDI program with the precaution that the long-term research character of the program should be preserved.

The title of this section has been chosen in order to highlight the fact that all three factors—mission, systems, and technology—should be considered together in discussing the feasibility and utility of BMD. They are closely coupled, interrelated pieces of the strategic defense puzzle. If any one of these three factors is considered in isolation, errors in judgment or ill-founded conclusions will result, which will detract from the quality of discussion.

By "mission" we mean the targets BMD is designed to defend, the threat it must meet, and the defense objective to be attained. BMD is commonly considered today, in the SDI debate, to have the mission of defending cities against a massive Soviet ballistic missile attack with the essential objective of damage denial. Alternatively, BMD is tasked with defending military targets against a massive Soviet attack, with the objective of damage limitation. Other missions, for damage denial, such as defending against an Nth country attack (any country other than the USSR, such as Libya), or accidental or unauthorized launch, are not as prominent today, though they have been studied in the past. Still another class of BMD mission is to defend time-dependent targets, such as SAC bases, with the objective of "buying time"—that is, escape time—for SAC bombers.

This is not the place to belabor the fairly obvious definitions of the various systems and technologies involved in each mission. I will take a moment to offer a couple of observations on the consideration of these factors in the current SDI debate. One is that systems are frequently proposed for use in the near term, when their constituent technology requirements cannot realistically be met in that timeframe. A certain amount of this is acceptable, if the proper qualifications are given—particularly that a crash effort is envisioned to accelerate the development of a particular set of technologies of high importance. However, careless proposals to bring about radical system solutions on a timescale completely out of the bounds of experience with complex weapons are misleading at best. They often lead to discussions about the relative merits of two different systems for the same timeframe, when the probability of their realization in the same period is so remote as to render the comparison meaningless.

Another misleading practice is to equate technical innovation with exotic systems. Enormous technical improvement can and should be made within the framework of more or less traditional BMD systems. In fact, some of the most promising technologies on the horizon can elevate traditional systems to levels of effectiveness and reliability which were previously unattainable. The field of data processing, discussed below, is an example of a technology which gets at the weakest link in earlier BMD systems, and which is now expanding at such a rapid rate that the challenge is how to harness it intelligently in advanced system designs. So pervasive is the impact of advanced data processing techniques that it is no longer necessary or proper to restrict our consideration to future developments, such as directed energy weapons.

The Importance of What Is Being Defended

The greatest confusion among the three factors of mission, systems, and technology relates to the blurring of distinctions about systems and technology demands for the missions of population defense on the one hand and military target defense on the other. This is probably caused in part because SDI began with an exclusive concentration on population defense, and has of late begun to swing toward interim military target defense. The mindset at the beginning, which was correct, was that major strides would have to be made in BMD systems and technology for population defense; that mindset has, however, mistakenly carried over to military target defense. There is a compelling case to be made that the traditional end of the spectrum of SDI systems, terminal and midcourse tiers of defense, are ideal for defense of military targets. While it is true that the level of defense of such targets will benefit from the later development of a boost-phase tier, when the attack will be thinned and the stress of enormous numbers of targets will be relieved, it is not necessary to await such development to prepare an effective early hedge option.

It is commonplace to read today the assertion—or more likely, the strong implication—that any defense mission considered for the near term must accept the limitations of inadequate technology and marginal cost-effectiveness. The conventional wisdom is that all defense missions must await the fruits of long-term SDI research in order to be technically and economically feasible. There is a pervasive attitude that "you can do it today, by brute force, but you can do it much better when radically new system concepts prove to be feasible." In point of fact, the major technical strides required are for city defense, the mission which defies the traditional approach to BMD. There are no significant, first-order factors of improved defense leverage lurking in the SDI program that will spell the difference between feasibility and infeasibility in the defense of military targets. The *raison d'être* for the long term is the mission of city defense.

Traditional systems are naturally well-adapted to the defense of military "point" targets: they effectively capitalize on cost-saving firing doctrines, and they exploit the advantages of proximity to the targets and the filtering effects of the atmosphere. It is fortunate that this is the case: The U.S. targets which are the most likely to be attacked in the near term correspond to those which can be feasibly defended by near-term systems and technology.

In an article in 1981, I argued the case that BMD had progressed to the point that effective defense of military targets, particularly ICBM silos, was confidently achievable.[45] By contrast, I noted it was not possible to make the same case for city defense. Fortunately, I did not make the prophecy so often heard today that city defense is impossible. I explained that "it is not intended to write off the feasibility of ultimately providing for city defense, particularly against light attacks . . . ." My main objective in writing this article was to contribute to an understanding of the three interrelated factors discussed above and, having made the point that defense of military targets was easier than city defense, go on to establish the fact that systems and technology were ripe for the former mission. It was a modest objective compared to the difficulties of arguing the ultimate success of SDI—which I believe is reachable—but it seemed to be worth tackling at the time.

In the article, I contrasted city defense with silo defense in order to simplify the discussion. City defense is the most difficult mission. "Silo defense" refers to defense of hardened ICBM sites (Minuteman or MX), the mission that has been analyzed more than any other—and the one that is less stressing than any other. All other missions, such as defense of SAC bases and the national command authority (NCA), fall between these two in terms of difficulty. The most important difference in these two missions

---

[45] William A. Davis, Jr., "Ballistic Missile Defense Will Work," *National Defense*, December 1981.

is that city defense requires a much higher level of effectiveness than silo defense. There are other differences, such as the fact that the "keepout zone" (the volume in space around a target where warheads must be denied penetration) for soft city targets is much larger than for hard silo targets, but they are subsidiary to the effectiveness level required in the economics of BMD.

The "leakage" of the BMD system (the percentage of attacking warheads that penetrate the defense and reach their target) for city defense must be extremely low (0-1 percent). The consequences of even one nuclear warhead getting through to a city are so great that this level of BMD effectiveness is essential. On the other hand, defense of hardened ICBM silos is "leakage tolerant"; that is, leakages of 10-50 percent can be allowed and still satisfy militarily significant defense goals. This difference in required effectiveness allows the use of a preferential defense firing doctrine for silo defense, a powerful tool to improve the leverage of defense in relation to offense.

In city defense, subtractive defense firing doctrine (sometimes called "first come, first served") is required, because none of the attacking nuclear warheads can be allowed to leak through. This means that one interceptor must be allocated for every warhead in the threat, a leverage ratio of 1:1 (the ratio of attacking warheads to defense interceptors). It may even be necessary to salvo interceptors at warheads to achieve the required kill probability, resulting in a leverage ratio of less than one. Preferential defense refers to the firing doctrine, adaptable to silo defense, of selecting certain targets (silos) in advance to be defended, while intentionally leaving others undefended. Obviously, this requires that the defense be able to sort out where all of the warheads are targeted; that is, the BMD system must be able to perform impact point prediction (a straightforward requirement for current terminal and midcourse sensors and data processors).

By way of illustration, consider the following example which demonstrates the advantages of preferential defense over subtractive defense. Against a given number of threatening warheads targeted on a number of silos, defended by a set number of defense interceptors, I showed that the outcome of an attack could be a difference of 50 percent survival versus 0 percent survival by applying preferential defense instead of subtractive defense. This simplified example glosses over many details, but it nevertheless gives an accurate picture of the power of preferential defense. Expressed in terms of leverage, the example shows that the 50 percent survival objective could be achieved with a leverage ratio of 2:1, twice as many attacking warheads as defense interceptors. This leverage is somewhat higher than can be realized in a more realistic scenario, but a leverage of 3:2 is reasonable. The fact that a defense objective can be achieved with fewer interceptors than attacking warheads is sometimes surprising to people hearing it for the first time. However, it is not mysterious if one grasps the basic idea of intentionally allowing some warheads to leak through to their targets, in order to conserve interceptors to defend other targets.

In defending deceptively based ICBM sites—such as MX in the Multiple Protective Structure (MPS) basing mode—the leverage of defense can be even higher than for defense of fixed sites. For the basing configurations studied by the Air Force several years ago, a single LoAD/Sentry interceptor could, theoretically, extract a leverage of about 20:1—that is, twenty attacking warheads for one interceptor. In actual deployment plans, the leverage turned out to be on the order of 7-10:1, still an impressive multiplier. This is primarily due to the compounding of leverages from preferential defense and deceptive basing. The result was achieved by deceptively basing the defense interceptor, as well as the MX missile, in one of the shelters of a twenty-shelter ring. The interceptor would pop up during an attack and preferentially defend the shelter containing the MX, thus doubling the attack price for killing an MX (40 warheads required rather than 20).

The experience of the studies of active defense combined with deceptive basing—although one of the basing modes got beyond the study phase—led me to believe that the ideal solution for ICBM vulnerability lies in a similar combination of basing schemes. Even with the leverage achievable with preferential defense, BMD systems are stressed in handling the enormous number of warheads and penetration aids postulated for future counterforce threats. Deception and mobility, of both the offensive and defensive components, greatly relieves the burden on a BMD system; conversely, BMD greatly improves the leverage achievable with deception and mobility. There seems to be some political or psychological barrier to the use of deception in the basing of strategic components. It is certainly attractive, however, from the point of view of cost-effectiveness.

Returning to the confusion surrounding BMD system and technology demands for city defense versus military target defense, it should be clear from the foregoing that the ability to employ a preferential firing doctrine for the latter mission is a critical differentiator. As shown, it can make a difference of at least 50 percent in the number of interceptors—the main determinant of total systems cost—required to satisfy a defense mission. Therefore, if the option of defending military targets is adopted early on, with city defense to follow along later, then such an option should be built upon components that can provide leverage to a preferential defense strategy. Components in this category are those which operate in the terminal and late midcourse regimes. By their very nature, space-based boost-phase weapons cannot readily, if at all, perform the accurate impact point prediction (IPP) required for preferential, discriminatory defense. (Sean K. Collins has recently authored an interesting article on preferential boost-phase defense, which appears to be useful for all boost-phase missions, but does not provide the IPP accuracy envisioned here.)[46] Remote from the targets being defended, they must be used during the first few minutes of the attack, when it is unclear exactly where the attacking ballistic missiles are targeted.

There are other reasons why it does not seem logical to consider space-based weapons for the near-term objective of military target defense. Chief among these are the facts that the technology is not sufficiently mature, and that the command-and-control problem is much more difficult. Even if one considers the use of kinetic energy weapons (KEW) in space versus directed energy weapons (DEW), the leadtime for developing and deploying such weapons has to be significantly greater than for ground-based terminal and late midcourse components. The problem of transporting the weapons to their stations in orbit—using the shuttle or expendable launch vehicles—would alone stretch leadtimes beyond that required for ground-based components. Furthermore, the command-and-control problem of remote, boost-phase weapons as compared to CONUS-based weapons is greater in technical difficulty, and farther away in potential availability. For near-term applications, there is a natural advantage in having defense weapons securely based on the ground, in the vicinity of the targets being defended. More time is available for viewing the threat and making decisions, and the allocation of defense resources is easier to handle if they are closer to the command authority. This is not to say that space-based assets such as surveillance and communication satellites could not contribute immensely to the engagement; rather, it is simply to say that the kill vehicles are best deployed on the ground for early defense missions.

Therefore, an evolutionary BMD deployment, sometimes referred to as "intermediate" or "transitional" deployment, is more naturally and logically conceived as one progressing from the ground up. The first step would be to defend key military targets with terminal and late midcourse defense components; the system could then grow gracefully toward city defense using space-based components.

---

[46] Sean K. Collins, "Preferential Boost-Phase Defense," *National Defense*, December 1985.

A Treaty-Compliant ATBM System

In Chapter 1, it was proposed that the terminal tier of an evolving layered defense system be developed as an ATBM system so as to satisfy dual missions, while remaining treaty-compliant for ATBM deployment. In a subsequent monograph, more will be written about the ATBM problem and approaches toward its solution. However, it is worth noting here that the two missions—ATBM and the bottom (or terminal) tier of a layered defense for CONUS—are close enough in technical requirements to be satisfied by the same terminal system. This was recognized by Fred Hoffman in his policy study, in which he listed ATM (he used the broader abbreviation to encompass cruise missiles) as one of a number of interesting intermediate deployment options.[47] As Hoffman also noted, it is reasonable to plan the later enhancement of such an initial terminal defense system with a midcourse overlay for either ATBM or CONUS deployment. For CONUS, an evolutionary deployment would also include a boost-phase tier when the technology becomes mature enough to support its deployment.

The concept of a dual-mission terminal BMD system has a precedent in the Soviet SA-X-12 system. *Soviet Military Power, 1985* notes that this system is "both a tactical SAM and antitactical ballistic missile . . . . the SA-10 and SA-X-12 may have the potential to intercept some types of U.S. strategic missiles as well."[48] Although the Soviets do not have as much incentive as the United States to develop a dual-mission system—having in the ABM-X-3 a rapidly deployable, terminal defense system already developed for strategic missiles—they clearly recognize the economies of dual-mission systems and the advantages of being able to deploy an ATBM system within the terms of the Treaty.

Studies in progress by the Army's Strategic Defense Command have considered dedicated ATBM system designs for countering various combinations of the tactical threats posed by the SS-21, SS-12 Mod 2, and SS-23 systems, as well as by the SS-20 intermediate-range ballistic missiles. In the studies, these tactical missiles were played against upgraded air defense systems (such as Patriot) and SDI components (such as HEDI/TIR), as well as against a dedicated ATBM system, in order to gain insight into the optimum composition of a defense system. While no final conclusion has been officially made, it appears that there is great merit in designing a dedicated ATBM system which can engage the full spectrum of TBMs, thus building in an inherent capability against strategic missiles. This capability comes about as a result of designing

---

[47] Hoffman, op. cit., p. 2.
[48] *Soviet Military Power, 1985,*op. cit., p. 48.

an ATBM system to engage the long-range SS-20, which has velocity and reentry characteristics similar to strategic missiles.

In brief, to assure a significant capability against strategic missiles in an ATBM system, one must select the right combination of interceptor velocity profile and radar power-aperture product for engaging the SS-20 end of the TBM spectrum, while observing size and weight constraints for component mobility. It appears that this is technically feasible. It will probably turn out that the resultant system is somewhat over-designed for the ATBM role, but this is not a serious penalty, especially when degrading factors such as electronic countermeasures (ECM) are considered. All indications suggest that careful design choices can lead to a versatile and lethal BMD system that would fill the gap for a near-term option.

Deployment Leadtime Reduction Profiles

How long would it take to develop a dual-capable terminal defense system, and what minimum deployment leadtime would be achievable? The many variables pertaining to this question make it difficult to answer precisely. However, I believe it is possible to arrive at a meaningful timeframe if some assumptions are made about the budget profile. In a paper I delivered at a Harvard BMD symposium in 1979, I included some leadtime and budgetary charts depicting three different kinds of pre-engineering development programs, each leading to different rates of leadtime reduction.[49] The three kinds of advanced development programs were:

- **System Prototype Demonstration/Optimum Budget.** This program reduced deployment leadtime (measured as years to IOC for every year of advanced development) at the greatest rate (about 1:1). Although it requires the largest peak budget, the total advanced development budget is the smallest of the three programs. For four to five years of advanced development, years to IOC can be reduced to a minimum of two to four years. (The Soviets have apparently exceeded this with their ABM-X-3 system, but it seems doubtful that with the required review and approval process, a U.S. program could duplicate the feat.)

- **Subsystem Advanced Development/Budget Constrained.** This type of program has a more shallow slope of years to IOC versus years in

[49] William A. Davis, Jr., "Current Technical Status of U.S. BMD Programs," *U.S. Arms Control Objectives and the Implications for Ballistic Missile Defense,* Proceedings of a Symposium held at the Center for Science and International Affairs, Harvard University, November 1-2, 1979, pp. 29-53.

advanced development, depending on the budget profile. While its peak budget is less than for full prototyping, its total budget is typically more. It is capable of bringing years to IOC down to the same minimum of two to four years, but with a longer period of advanced development—hence, the total leadtime is greater.

- **Advanced Technology/Level of Effort.** This kind of program is characterized by a curve of essentially zero slope. At the time I presented the paper, I had in mind the kind of advanced technology program that was carried out in the mid-1970s—that is, a flat curve, low-budget program. However, I believe the same essentially zero slope in leadtime reduction pertains to a high-budget-level program, such as SDI, when the nature of the development is not prototypical system development. In other words, there is a very long leadtime to potential IOC, too long to estimate confidently.

Given the seriousness of the BMD leadtime asymmetry now existing between the United States and the Soviet Union, it would be desirable to find a leadtime compression technique better than those outlined above. It is not encouraging to be left with the answer that a minimum total leadtime of about six years is the best that can be hoped for. (There are many professional BMD analysts who would argue that even that period is optimistic.) However, experience on past BMD programs indicates that even the most straightforward terminal defense system, given the highest program priority, would require at least this amount of time. Of course, one can always imagine national crises, outside our experience base, that might accelerate development to an unpredictable rate. Nevertheless, BMD systems have a built-in resistance to crash development because of their complexity and limited industrial base—now growing under SDI.

LoAD/Sentry System

In order to facilitate the development of a rapidly deployable terminal defense system, for both ATBM deployment and as a hedge option for CONUS deployment, it would be necessary to build on the experience and database of past terminal BMD systems. LoAD/Sentry, the last terminal BMD system development program, would provide a useful model for the size, operating characteristics, and technology required for a new terminal system. LoAD/Sentry was the third in a series of terminal system developments in the 1970s and early 1980s, following Safeguard and the Site Defense program. It incorporated a number of advanced design features that could be taken as a point of departure for the next generation system.

LoAD/Sentry was essentially a down-sized derivative of the predecessor Site Defense system. It followed a trend of going to smaller components that was started in the transition from Safeguard to Site Defense. Some observers hailed this trend as a miracle of miniaturization, but the main reason for the smaller size was considerably less dramatic. It was to enable the defense unit to be concealed in an MX shelter. In order to accomplish this deceptive basing, the components were scaled so that the radar was about 1/40th the size of the Site Defense Radar, while the interceptor was a single-stage system, about half the size of the Sprint II Site Defense interceptor.

As the name implies, LoAD/Sentry operated at very low altitudes; all functions are performed at altitudes lower than 50,000 feet, on a timeline of less than 10 seconds. Of course, this limits the defense applications to hard targets, such as the MX protective shelters, and it requires the defense components to be extremely resistant to nuclear effects. (Nuclear "hardness" was the driving technology requirement for LoAD/Sentry, especially the unprecedented "hardness" level required for the radar.) It is likely that an advanced terminal defense system, with the versatility to defend a range of NATO and CONUS military targets, would need to be larger and of longer range than LoAD/Sentry.

A significant feature of LoAD/Sentry that would be retained for an advanced system is its use of distributed data processing. This data processing approach promises to provide the required BMD computational power at lower cost than centralized, mainframe computers. It rests on the microcomputer revolution that has spawned the personal computer industry and dramatically reduced hardware cost as it relates to instruction execution rate. To illustrate this trend, third generation computers of the 1960s had a cost ratio of about one million dollars per MIPS (million of instructions per second); fourth generation machines reduced this to about one hundred thousand dollars per MIPS. Distributed data processing promises to reduce this further to one thousand dollars per MIPS or less.

In addition to the cost advantage, distributed data processing offers other significant advantages for advanced BMD systems. These include graceful growth through the addition of modular units, the ability to meet changing requirements through reconfiguration, and a high degree of fault tolerance through redundancy and other design techniques. These features were described in a forward-looking doctoral dissertation by Dr. Charles R. Vick, currently head of the Computer Science Department at Auburn University and a major contributer to progress in BMD data processing over the past fifteen years.[50] Although significant progress was made on the LoAd/Sentry program before its termination in 1984, much work remains to be done toward the perfection of a BMD distributed data processing system. It would not be accurate to portray this data processing approach as routine and straightforward; above all else, it requires a very thoughtful partitioning of the system components and functions in a way that has never before been reduced to practice.

The Eastport Study

A number of parallels to the distributed data processing approach can be seen in the recently completed "Eastport Study," prepared for the SDIO.[51] The panel appointed to conduct this ad hoc study was charged with devising "an appropriate computational/communication response to the [SDI battle management computing] problem and make recommendations for a research and technology program to implement the response." The panel's conclusions were generally positive with respect to the feasibility of this massive data processing undertaking, but recommended technical and management approaches that were somewhat unconventional. The panel expressed a preference for a relatively decentralized system architecture, less dependent on tight coordination and generally consistent with a distributed data processing approach.

One characteristic of distributed data processing was picked up and amplified by the Eastport Study as a major aspect of their recommended approach. They recommended the liberal use of advanced computer hardware, exploiting the technologies of very high speed integrated circuits (VHSIC) and very large-scale integration (VLSI), to simplify software development. Frequently in the past the opposite approach has been taken—that is, software has been honed in order to relieve the demands on hardware. The software development job is so challenging for SDI that the panel felt faster computation should be employed whenever possible, allowing the use of simple algorithms and reliable software methodology.

The Gloomy Parnas Prognosis

Much of the technical debate on the feasibility of SDI revolves around the data processing requirements, particularly the software. David L. Parnas is probably the best-known professional skeptic on the feasibility of successfully developing the software for a full-scale SDI system. He

---

[50] Charles R. Vick, "A Dynamically Reconfigurable Distributed Computing System," Ph.D. Dissertation, Auburn University, December 13, 1979.

[51] Eastport Study Group, *A Report to the Director, Strategic Defense Initiative Organization,* December 1985.

from the SDIO Panel on Computing in Support of Battle Man-
and subsequently wrote a paper explaining his resignation,
which contained eight short essays on why he thought SDI software was
unattainable.[52] He is Lanscowne Professor of Computer Science at the
University of Victoria, and has an impressive background of software
research both in the academic community and in U.S. defense applications. His extremely pessimistic assessment of the feasibility of SDI
software was thus accorded considerable respect, if not ready agreement,
within the larger SDI community of government and contractor personnel.

It is not practical here to provide a full summary of Parnas's criticism. Of
his eight essays, most of which discuss the state of general software
engineering development, the one which merits the greatest attention
addresses the unique properties of SDI software. Here he characterizes
both the threat and the SDI components themselves as so uncertain in
characteristics and behavior as to defy control by battle management
software. He states that it will be impossible to test the SDI software, that
it will not be amenable to human intervention or debugging, and that the
battle management software will have to control a fluid and growing
number of software systems embedded in the constituent weapons and
sensors. The net effect of his position is to raise doubts that the software
can be reliably developed, independent of its size. It would seem that
the unconventional approaches recommended by the Eastport Panel,
which avoid the pitfalls of extrapolating from the experience of other large
software development projects, are necessary to answer the criticism of
Parnas.

It seems worthy of note, as a historical footnote, that the computer hardware and software for the Safeguard system were successfully developed
in the face of intense criticism that it could not be done. Even though it
was not nearly as complex as the data processing requirements for SDI,
it was, at the time, a system which required the development of the first
practical multiprocessor (there were no commercial computers on the
market which could do the job) and "one of the most complicated real-
time software systems ever conceived . . . . "[53] During the late 1960s,
many experts—including a special committee of the American Academy
of Science—predicted that the multiprocessor could not meet the throughput
requirements (MIPS). But in final Safeguard tests, the multiprocessors
followed a linear increase in MIPS for up to eight parallel processors (an

---

[52] David L. Parnas, "Software Aspects of Strategic Defense Systems," *American Scientist*,
September-October 1985.

[53] *ABM Research and Development at Bell Laboratories, Project History*, prepared by Bell
Laboratories on behalf of Western Electric, Whippany, New Jersey, October 1975, p. I-
50.

achievement which defied predictions that the increase would be highly nonlinear and very small after 4-5 processors were paralleled) and exceeded design goals. Moreover, the Safeguard software, even though its development was marked by a number of setbacks and substantial cost, performed reliably—twenty-four hours per day, seven days per week—in the tactical site at Grand Forks, North Dakota.

Endoatmospheric Nonnuclear Kill

Before leaving the "lessons learned" from LoAD/Sentry, and the suitability of its features for a modern terminal defense system, it should be noted that its nuclear-tipped interceptor would have to be replaced by a nonnuclear interceptor. As previously noted, I share Dr. Teller's view that the objective technical arguments lead to the selection of a low-yield nuclear warhead for a terminal defense system. However, the political arguments against such a system are so powerful that I do not see how it could gain approval. This is particularly true for NATO deployment, where there is increasing interest in an ATBM capability against nonnuclear TBM warheads. Dr. Manfred Woerner, the Minister of Defense of the Federal Republic of Germany, has written that the ATBM system would be "directed primarily against conventionally-armed missiles; therefore, a nuclear defense—especially to the extent that it might entail first-use of nuclear munitions—is out of the question."[54]

The main reason I am concerned about the use of nonnuclear warheads for terminal defense (that is, for endoatmospheric operation) is that it is exceedingly difficult to achieve the small-miss distances required to obtain a high single-shot kill probability with nonnuclear warheads. A great deal of research on endoatmospheric nonnuclear kill has been conducted by the Strategic Defense Command for about the last ten years, and substantial progress has been made. (Similar research was conducted by the BMD Advanced Technology Center before the creation of the Strategic Defense Command.) However, the problem is much more difficult than exoatmospheric nonnuclear kill, as successfully demonstrated in the Homing Overlay Experiment (HOE). Atmospheric slowdown creates, in effect, a maneuvering target. This stresses all aspects of the guidance and control problem. The preferred guidance approaches are semiactive or active radar homing. In particular, a great deal of research has been devoted to millimeter wave active homing, in which the use of short wavelengths allows the utilization of small apertures to achieve the required angular resolution.

---

[54] Manfred Woerner, "A Missile Defense for NATO Europe," *Strategic Review*, Winter 1986.

I would not want to present a net assessment of endoatmospheric non-nuclear kill that is unduly pessimistic. In fact, I am confident it will prove to be feasible for a nonresponsive threat. However, there are at least two potential responses by the offense that must be met if a robust capability is to be obtained: salvage fuzing and the maneuverable reentry vehicle (MARV). Salvage fuzing refers to the offensive tactic of detonating nuclear warheads upon encountering the nonnuclear defensive burst. (Note that this technique is not applicable for defending against conventional TBMs.) The resultant nuclear effects could cause damage to the defended targets and create a nuclear blackout of the defense. MARV would be a threat to the capabilities of a nonnuclear terminal interceptor because it would contribute significantly to larger miss distances—and hence, lower kill probability. There are defensive countermoves to both of these offensive responses, but the advantage in this game tilts in favor of the offense. For this reason, again, it would be prudent to design a low-yield nuclear backup, at least for the CONUS application of an advanced terminal defense system.

The Site Defense System

The Site Defense System was the principal BMD system under development prior to LoAD/Sentry. It was intended to be fully prototyped, and prototype models of its radar and data processing subsystems were built and tested at Kwajalein Missile Range. The Sprint II interceptor, designed for Site Defense, was not built and tested because of budget limitations. The contributions of the Site Defense program to the demonstration of the system-level performance of a terminal BMD system, in defense of military targets against large threats, has never been fully recognized. It concentrated on the most critical issues associated with this mission, and systematically demonstrated—in live tests and simulations—that it was feasible to build a system capable of doing the job. The main issues it addressed are of continuing significance: discrimination and bulk filtering, operation in a nuclear environment, real-time software development, factory assembly techniques for phased-array radars, and survivability of the defense components.

The first of these critical issues, discrimination, is so profoundly important to the technical and economic feasibility of BMD that it merits further discussion later. However, it is instructive first to address briefly two transitional periods in BMD history: from Safeguard to Site Defense, and from Site Defense to LoAD/Sentry. In the latter transition, a layered defense system was studied seriously for the first time, and the influence of this concept is very prevalent today.

Transition from Safeguard to Site Defense

The Safeguard system, the main components of which were originally designed for city defense, was not ideally matched to the mission of defending military targets. This fact was recognized by the Safeguard Program Manager in 1969, General Starbird. Starbird was an outstanding program manager who exercised enormous power and authority in the Safeguard era (reminiscent of Admiral Raborn and the Polaris). He headed a massive organization of government and industrial personnel charged with deploying the nation's first BMD system, and he controlled a budget that peaked at over one billion dollars per year in the early 1970s. It is a tribute to his vision and objectivity that he recognized that the Safeguard system was large, cumbersome, and costly for the mission of defending Minuteman, the number one priority under the Safeguard charter announced by President Nixon in March 1969.

In September 1969, General Starbird requested that I chair an ad hoc study to investigate alternative defense concepts for defending Minuteman, in comparison with Safeguard. The eight-week study, called Minuteman Defense Study I (or "MDS I"; there was to be an "MDS II" and "MDS III"), was conducted with the participation of a number of government agencies and perhaps a dozen companies, notably General Research Corporation (GRC) and Riverside Research Institute (RRI). The Bell Telephone Laboratories (BTL) team, in addition to its massive effort on the Safeguard system, had also conducted studies on advanced systems for Minuteman defense, and these systems were included in the scope of MDS I. The advanced systems defined by BTL were called VIRADE and HSD. VIRADE (Virtual Radar Deployment) was a concept for deceptively basing the radars of a defense system to minimize their vulnerability to attack. HSD (Hardsite Defense) was the fixed version of VIRADE. In addition to these concepts, other popular concepts were thrown into the hopper, and a few new defense concepts were synthesized during the course of the study. Ten concepts in all were comparatively evaluated.

Several significant findings came out of the MDS I study, leading toward the initiation of the Site Defense Program (following MDS II, and with many excursions in between). Perhaps the most important finding of MDS I was that the ideal system for Minuteman defense should be sized to handle the threat with a third-generation commercial computer (equivalent to the CDC 7600). This would have allowed trading on the commercial computer market in the event the system was deployed, and would have supported the targeted IOC in the late 1970s. Following from this sizing constraint was the design of a deployment ratio (number of Minuteman silos per radar) of about seven to one. Until this time, deployment ratios of seventeen to one (requiring a fourth-generation computer) and one to one (requiring a modest computer but a lot of radars and computers, hence a costly solution) had been considered, but nothing in between. This seven-to-one optimum was driven mainly by the fact that the largest coverage (deployment ratio) possible was desirable from a cost standpoint, so long as the local traffic could be handled by the radar/computer defense unit.

Around 1970, then, the stage was set for a transition from Safeguard to Site Defense—in the event that further deployment for Minuteman defense was authorized. No decision was made to broaden the deployment in the 1970-1972 period; ultimately, the ABM Treaty intervened in 1972 to make the question academic. Following the treaty-imposed limitation on deployment, Site Defense was defined as a prototype demonstration program and begun as a long-term development program.

The Army-Air Force BMD Debate

During the Army's concept formulation phase for Site Defense, the Air Force advanced a competitive concept for Minuteman defense called Mohawk. Mohawk was a derivative of the Hawk air defense system, featuring the use of a nonnuclear warhead and a deployment ratio of one to one (a radar for every Minuteman silo). Air Force spokesmen argued that their concept would be more economical for Minuteman defense, and that it could be better integrated into their existing command and control structure. The most controversial aspect of the Air Force concept was the feasibility of achieving high lethality against ICBM reentry vehicles with homing guidance and nonnuclear warheads. As previously noted, endoatmospheric nonnuclear kill is a challenging technical objective even today, and the Air Force was claiming its achievability in the early 1970s with an existing system.

The competition between the Army and Air Force on approaches to Minuteman defense became increasingly intense. Someone in the Pentagon conceived the idea of staging a technical debate between the Services to determine which concept was superior. The Air Force proposal had sparked the first eruption of an inter-Service "roles and missions battle" over BMD since the time of the Wizard/Nike-Zeus competition between the same two Services in the 1955-1958 period. Moreover, it led to the first attempt to have the technical combatants resolve their own differences. The debate was held in the Hoffman Building on the Washington Beltway, staffed by about ten permanent technical personnel on each side as well as other specialists who shuttled in and out on special topics. General John Toomay chaired the Air Force side and Julian Davidson chaired the Army side. Predictably, the weeks of ensuing discussion did not result in agreement, nor even a perceptible convergence toward a preferred approach. The Army held fast to the argument that the nuclear site defense system, with a deployment ratio of about seven to one, was the most effective and economical concept; the Air Force stuck with an evolving concept of single silo, nonnuclear defense. There were lengthy forays into just about every major technical issue of BMD, such as bulk filtering and discrimination, and there were sophisticated costing exercises on both sides that disagreed even more than the technical discussions. Toward the end of this unique debate there was a weary awareness by all concerned that it was hopelessly bogged down in a mass of conflicting technical data and cost figures.

To the great relief of both sides of the debate, the deadlock was broken by a Pentagon decision that had nothing whatever to do with the complex technical battles being waged in the Hoffman Building. The Chief of Staff of the Air Force wrote a letter, the net effect of which was a total capitulation by the Air Force. The motivation for the letter was to escape the potential budgetary consequences to the Air Force of "winning" the debate and being thus required to channel R&D dollars into BMD development. The higher levels of the Air Force were at the time much more interested in maintaining an adequate budget for other strategic programs, particularly for the manned bomber. They had scant interest in taking over a strategic defense program that had a large appetite for development dollars and a small base of support in the Congress. The Army thus won the BMD debate by default, and proceeded over the next several years to develop Site Defense—and to wage a constant battle to maintain Congressional support in a treaty-limited environment.

The Transition from Site Defense to LoAD/Sentry: Layered Defense

The transition period between Site Defense and LoAD/Sentry included an intensive analysis of layered defense. However, that work remained relatively obscure for reasons which are difficult to identify. By way of background, the extension of BMD's reach into the exoatmospheric, midcourse regime had been explored in various studies, data gathering programs, and demonstration programs conducted by BMD advanced technology organizations (ABMDA and BMDATC) going back to the late 1960s. Typical of the studies performed on midcourse, exoatmospheric defense were the Indian Summer Study of 1969—which took into account most of the penetration aids and defense responses heard today—and the Light Area Defense Study of 1973, which sparked the Congressional reaction noted in Chapter 2. Data gathering programs, emphasizing the acquisition of long wavelength infrared (LWIR) signature data, included FAIR (fly-along infrared), SCOOP (Strategic Technology Office, Confirmation of Phenomenology), SOFT (signature of fragmented tanks), and DOT (designating optical tracker). The most notable example of a demonstration program was HOE.

While exoatmospheric, midcourse defense was, and continues to be, less mature than terminal defense, it had come along to a point in the late 1970s that it was considered a strong candidate for autonomous defense, or as the upper layer of a two-tiered system. The concept was to have two sequential layers of defense, with either the Site Defense System or LoAD/Sentry as the underlay. McDonnell Douglas Corporation, which was the major BMD system development contractor at this time, performed detailed system definition and trade-off studies of layered defense. The fundamental advantage of layered defense over a single-tier defense was in the lower leakage obtainable (if the overlay had a leakage of 20 percent and the underlay had a leakage of 20 percent, the combined leakage would be the product of the two, or 4 percent). The overlay part of the layered defense concept featured a midcourse interceptor with multiple nonnuclear warheads, and a large optical sensor on the bus to perform target designation for the kill vehicles. The concept proved to be extremely effective in the Minuteman defense and other missions.

The system analysis of layered defense revealed a surprising degree of resilience to increasing threat levels and penetration tactics. Because of its low leakage and low cost per intercept using multiple nonnuclear midcourse kill vehicles, the marginal cost of the defense was estimated to be less than that of the offense. Using "adaptive" preferential defense tactics, where the defense was assumed capable of surveying the entire threat complex and allocating interceptors accordingly, an unprecedented degree of defense leverage was achievable. The use of dual-phenomenology sensors in the system (optics and radar) greatly improved the resistance to penetration aids, because of the difficulty of designing penetration aids that are effective against both types of sensors. Overall, the layered defense concept was the most robust concept that had been devised until the late 1970s.

Recent design concepts for a midcourse system, in the context of the SDI architecture studies, use the ERIS (exoatmospheric reentry vehicle interceptor subsystem) interceptor with designation either from the AOA (airborne optical adjunct) or from satellites. The ERIS interceptor is conceptually traceable to the Fletcher Panel's call for cheap, dumb midcourse interceptors. It has replaced the larger, more costly midcourse interceptors originally envisioned, which contained small multiple interceptors and their own designation sensors. There are a number of reasons why the ERIS concept is attractive, especially the fact that its small size will allow it to be mobile. It may well be that the mobility feature is essential for the defense of NATO-Europe against tactical ballistic missiles. However, there are a number of reasons why the ERIS concept may not be as suitable for CONUS defense as the larger, multiple warhead interceptor concept.

Designating ERIS interceptors from either an aircraft or satellite platform is difficult due to the small error "basket" required for such "dumb" interceptors. By contrast, the earlier midcourse interceptor concept could be easily designated to a sector, within which its own D3 sensor could perform fine-grained tracking as the basis for designating its multiple-kill vehicles. More importantly, its onboard sensor could better perform the close-in discrimination so critical to efficient allocation of interceptors. It is inherently more difficult to discriminate at the longer range of an aircraft platform, or the even longer range of a satellite platform. Another major trade-off that may still favor a multiple-kill vehicle midcourse interceptor is the cost per intercept. Even though it is a high priority objective to drive down the unit cost of ERIS, the use of small-kill vehicles (derivatives of the HOE kill vehicle or the HIT vehicle) lofted by a "mother" interceptor may result in a cost advantage.

Another system design issue related to the midcourse tier is its relative dependence on space-based sensors. While it seems highly desirable to employ space sensors for many BMD functions, the crucial question is how to respond if space-based sensors do not survive. The optical probe is one response which has been under study for a number of years, and is a promising concept for second-line sensors in the event space sensors are knocked out. Basically, it is an optical sensor on top of a rocket. It can be placed on station very rapidly to designate midcourse interceptors, and thereby prevent the calamity that, if the space-based sensors are lost, the stockpile of interceptors would remain in their holes unused.

Ironically, most of the criticism of the earlier layered defense concept related to its complexity. At the time it was being briefed to various groups around the country—including the Defense Science Board, the National Security Council, and the JASONS (a group of university professors who consult for the Defense Department's Office of Research and Engineering)—a common impression was that its complexity would defy effective solution of the battle-management and command/control problems. By today's standards, and in comparison to the complexity of SDI, the layered defense concept was relatively straightforward. As previously discussed, it comprises the lower two tiers of currently-envisioned SDI architectures in which all the interceptors are ground-based. It represents the first two steps in the evolutionary deployment plan advocated in this study.

Discrimination

The dominant technical issue in the earlier layered defense concept, and a continuing issue in the SDI program, is discrimination. Discrimination, in the simplest terms, is the ability of a defense system to differentiate between real targets and other objects such as penetration aids and debris. Conventionally, the level of estimated discrimination capability for a defense system is expressed as a "K factor," where the larger the value of K, the better the discrimination capability. The K factor was derived at MIT's Lincoln Laboratories as a convenient tool to measure statistically how well the characteristics of two objects, such as a warhead and a decoy, can be differentiated. The implications of discrimination for the effectiveness of the defense system are expressed by two kinds of errors: the error of calling a warhead a decoy (probability of leakage), and the error of calling a decoy a warhead (probability of false alarm). Both of these errors can be minimized by enforcing a large K factor, and for a given K factor the defense performs trade-offs between the two classes of error; that is, the defense has the option of making leakage low at the expense of high false alarms, and vice versa.

If the problem of discrimination is examined for the various tiers of an SDI architecture, reasonable judgments can be made about how well it can be solved. In the boost-phase, discrimination is not a problem in the conventional sense, as it is not practical to replicate large ballistic missile boosters with penetration aids. There are other countermeasures—such as fast-burn boosters—which must be contended with in the boost phase, but not conventional penetration aids. In the terminal phase, the radar database relevant to discrimination is relatively large, and the development of discrimination techniques has progressed to the point of demonstration in simulations and field tests. The Site Defense Program, in particular, demonstrated the efficacy of terminal discrimination in a systems context. The Site Defense system tested at Kwajalein had several discrimination algorithms embedded in its software, and it showed that sequential, real-time discrimination was achievable to the degree required for cost-effective terminal defense. The problem of midcourse, exoatmospheric defense is the most difficult to solve, and the associated technology is immature when compared to terminal defense.

Midcourse defense, unlike terminal defense, does not have the atmosphere to aid discrimination. Most terminal defense discrimination depends on the atmosphere to slow down the threat objects and create visible wakes behind them. In midcourse defense, other threat observables—such as radiant intensity—must be used by the defense as a basis for discrimination. It is inherently easier to design penetration aids against a midcourse defense system, which is entirely dependent on passive optical measurements for discrimination. Examples of such countermeasures include balloons and aerosols. For this reason, it appears likely that the midcourse tier of SDI will require the use of other discrimination techniques. Candidate techniques include imaging sensors in space, and active and interactive devices to probe the objects in the threat cloud.

Recent study results of complete SDI systems indicate that discrimination capability is a dominant factor in total system cost. The sensitivity of total system cost to midcourse discrimination capability—particularly between a range of K values of two to three—is so great that the economic feasibility of the defense may well rest on the achievement of a level of capability on the upper side of this range. When this sensitivity is plotted as a function of cost versus number of space weapons used in the boost phase (for different values of K) it becomes clear that the use of such space weapons acts to reduce the cost penalty of poor discrimination. However, the cost regime where this occurs is so high that it raises the fundamental question of whether poor discrimination can ever be economically acceptable. The evidence suggests that a minimum threshold level of midcourse discrimination capability must be achieved to minimize cost. If this is achieved, space-based weapons do not provide a large cost payoff.

The above discussion tends to oversimplify a complex set of interactions. One facet of this is a question of numbers. The midcourse tier of a defense system is confronted with such a staggering number of objects in a typical scenario that it is problematic whether it can realistically cope with the traffic. The functions of acquisition, scan-to-scan correlation, and tracking will be difficult to perform without succumbing to saturation—even before the question of discrimination is faced. Therefore, the use of boost-phase weapons to thin the attack may be mandatory.

The Absentee Ratio

Another strong driver in the economics of a full-scale SDI system, responsible for some of the trends discussed above, is the "absentee ratio" for space-based components. The absentee ratio is defined as the total number of satellites in a constellation as related to the number that are in position to enter into an engagement during the launch window. This number has been at the center of a great deal of controversy concerning the efficiency and cost of SDI systems. Most of the controversy has stemmed from the various means used to calculate the number of satellites required to obtain continuous coverage of the threatening ICBM launch sites, a number that has varied from 2,400 down to about 100. The lower number is closer to the actual number required, and is supported by most analysts today.

In the earlier discussion of the interaction of total system cost, number of space weapons, and midcourse discrimination capability, the lower range of satellites required was assumed and, therefore, the absentee ratio was minimized. Even so, it is costly to use space-based weapons, and there is a strong incentive to improve midcourse discrimination in order to reduce system cost. In a different sense, terminal defense systems also have an absentee ratio, owing to their relatively small footprint (area of coverage). A large number of terminal defense units is required to cover a target set spread over an extensive geographical area. In this respect, midcourse defense is the only tier that effectively combines the advantages of large areas of coverage with small absentee ratios. Again, this line of reasoning leads to the conclusion that the key to economical defense is strengthening the capability of the midcourse tier, ideally by removing its discrimination weakness.

Most of this chapter has addressed the more traditional BMD systems and the relatively prosaic technologies of data processing and discrimination. Not much has been written about exotic technologies. This is because I have been mostly concerned about advocating a shift in SDI emphasis toward the near term. However, I would like to underscore my support for the application of directed energy weapons to BMD, a position dating back to my first association with the Army high-energy laser program in 1961. Although it was not a continuous period of involvement, I was fortunate to be part of the later cycle of research on free electron lasers (FELS) and neutral particle beams in the Army BMD Advanced Technology Center during the 1970s. I am among those who believe that the required brightness and other characteristics of these devices will be achieved, so that extremely lethal directed energy weapons will be created within a few years. However, the effect of the absentee ratio, and other problems associated with space basing, cause me to believe that the relay basing mode (ground-based lasers, such as FELs, with relay and fighting mirrors in space) is preferable to space basing.

4. The Strategic Environment

The Synergy of Different Forms of Strategic Defense

It has often been noted that the Soviets are more "defense oriented" than the United States. They place a greater value on strategic defense weapons to protect their homeland from attack by any means. The United States tends to subscribe to a different theory—exemplified by earlier quotations of Talbott and Manatt—that a good offense is the best defense. I attempted in Chapter 2 to contrast the doctrines of assured destruction and damage limitation that codify these differences in U.S. and Soviet philosophy. But a more tangible measure is the hardware, the "brick and mortar," each side has built for offensive and defensive purposes. The Soviets have clearly built more strategic defense systems than the United States; moreover, they have national networks of such systems in place, including air defense, BMD, civil defense, and space defense.

I will not elaborate here the details of Soviet systems for strategic defense. A wealth of information is available on these systems from many sources, such as the annual Department of Defense document, *Soviet Military Power*.[55] My purpose here is to discuss how the resulting environment makes a difference to the future of the Soviet BMD program, and to contrast that with the environment under which the U.S. SDI program will be carried out. I will first examine the more direct implications of the Soviet defense environment for the relative effectiveness of future BMD systems, and then discuss their indirect effects on program stability and organizations.

With respect to system effectiveness, it is necessary to treat the role of BMD in concert with other defense systems to obtain a realistic measure of the BMD contribution. Since there are a multiplicity of strategic offensive weapons that are used in any postulated exchange, the defenses against all of these weapons must be taken into account. Earlier, I commented on the relative advantage the Soviets enjoy in BMD by virtue of the fact that they design for a retaliatory strike rather than a first strike. Similarly, they have a large potential advantage by combining BMD with air and civil defense systems already in place. There is a striking difference in the contribution of BMD to overall limitation of damage if it is deployed as an integral part of an existing defense environment as opposed to its deployment in isolation.

---

[55] *Soviet Military Power, 1985*, op. cit., p. 43.

A common way of showing the effect of a Soviet breakout BMD deployment is to plot graphs that portray net damage as a function of different assumed levels of effectiveness of their air defense, civil defense, and BMD systems. Passive measures employed by the Soviets, such as hardening of facilities and fallout shelters, are commonly portrayed at a certain fixed level of effectiveness. Then their massive air defense forces are plotted parametrically for different assumed attrition levels of our manned bombers and cruise missiles. Superimposed on these two types of defenses is the relative contribution of BMD systems for different assumed levels of effectiveness.

BMD exhibits a high degree of leverage when plotted in the context of a combined defense network, as described above. Even a modest BMD capability makes a significant contribution to reduction of net damage. BMD has a disproportionate contribution if it is the last ingredient in a total strategic defense mix. This fact provides another reason—quite apart from their apparent approach of designing against a retaliatory strike— why the Soviets are interested in BMD systems that provide only modest capability. It also lends credence to the argument that they have a strong incentive to break out from the ABM Treaty and deploy a nationwide BMD system. BMD is the only missing link in their defenses against nuclear attack.

The Influence of the Political Environment on Program Stability

Another result of a general political and strategic environment firmly rooted in the precept that "defense is good" is its favorable influence on program stability. Since the Soviets have never been ambivalent about the desirability (and indeed the necessity) of building strategic defenses, their strategic defense programs have been stable and continuous.

In the parlance of strategic analysts, there are two forms of strategic stability—crisis stability and arms control stability. A different kind of stability is introduced here—program stability—that should not be confused with these other terms. It has nothing to do with the larger issues of whether BMD is strategically stabilizing or destabilizing; it has a great deal to do with how productive a BMD program can be over a long period. In Chapter 2, I traced some of the history of BMD, in order to provide a glimpse of the cycles which the program has undergone over the past twenty years. The program has operated in a turbulent environment, marked by two large-scale national debates in the late 1960s and the mid-1980s.

It is instructive to look at both long-term and short-term cycles in the BMD program in order to appreciate the stability problem. I have discussed the long-term cycle from a concentration on a national deployment (Safeguard) to a strong swing toward long-term research emphasis, followed by a later peak of emphasis on short-term deployment readiness. I have also mentioned short-term cycles from interest in extremely primitive BMD concepts to highly exotic concepts, which have at times been concurrent. From the policy level, I have characterized the recurrence of cycles in support for long-term and short-term research, and the difficulties of tailoring a development program to be responsive to these cycles. These cycles are particularly debilitating to the BMD program because BMD development is essentially a long-term business; it takes a long time to carry out any worthwhile experiment or significant research task.

In the past, major BMD experiments or demonstration programs seem to have had a gestation period of about seven years. Some of the current SDI projects may take even longer to come to fruition. Typically, a lot of money is spent and a lot of people are tied up on such programs before anything happens. Decisionmakers in the chain of command become impatient because of the lack of visible results; funding support invariably wanes as the program matures. Sometimes there is a change in administration during the life cycle of a major program; there are always changes in key players who must be resold on the merits of the program. Meanwhile, there must be a champion and a team of fiercely loyal "believers" in the program if it is to survive.

To illustrate the point, I will briefly recount two major BMD experiments— one an abysmal failure and the other a roaring success.

The SOFT (signature of fragmented tanks) program was planned as a program to gather signature data on an ICBM liquid booster tank which had been deliberately blown apart prior to reentry. It was considered that such a tactic was one that could be readily exercised by a potential attacker without requiring a great deal of technological know-how or a long leadtime. The program originated in the Pentagon and it was handed down to the Army BMD organization in the early 1970s for implementation. It enjoyed considerable priority and funding support because of the high level of its origin, as well as the fact that it tied into the then-popular mission of light area defense.

The wheels of project organization and source selection turned fairly rapidly on SOFT, and a prime contractor was picked to conduct the experiment. As the experiment design unfolded, the program underwent typical increases in complexity and stretchout. It involved the firing of a Titan ICBM out of Vandenberg which had primer cord precisely wrapped around its second stage to create fragments upon detonation that were controlled in direction, velocity, and spin rate. An optical probe was to be fired at Kwajalein to gather optical data on the fragment cloud, the primary objective, and the radars at the range were to gather microwave signature data. In one span of about three months between program reviews, the program suffered a 30 percent budget overrun—another standard feature of such programs. Another event, not so standard, was a 40 percent cut in the ABMDA budget, which contained the SOFT project. (This was the previously described Congressional cut, associated with displeasure over Light Area Defense.) The cut occurred at about the midpoint of the project's life cycle. SOFT began to reel from guilt by association, and support for the program rapidly dissipated—which always happens when a program is financially wounded.

One of the adjustments that had to be made in the SOFT program because of budget cuts proved to be fatal—the reduction in number of flights from several to one. When the one mission was finally conducted, there was a failure in the optical sensor on the probe (actually, a software error that caused premature sensor uncapping) that resulted in the failure to acquire optical signature data. While the secondary objectives of creating the fragment cloud and obtaining radar data were successful, the primary objective of obtaining optical data was not met. It was a dismal outcome for a long program, costing about $20 million; moreover, because the support for the objectives had disappeared, there was no opportunity for recovery. The original supporters of SOFT in the Pentagon had left by the time the experiment had failed, so there was no one there to share the blame.

There are many morals and lessons to be learned from SOFT. For present purposes, the changes of fads and fashions in BMD politics, projected threats, and national missions will be mentioned as factors contributing to its demise. While it was a victim of an unusual confluence of destructive forces, its life cycle had many features which are typical of any major experiment. Basically, it was at risk of losing support because it took a long time to conduct. The constituency required to sustain a project rarely lasts for more than two or three years.

The second example is the Homing Overlay Experiment (HOE). When this experiment was first proposed in the Pentagon—involving the interception of a mock-up of an ICBM nuclear warhead with a nonnuclear defensive warhead—it was turned down. The reason given for rejection was that it could be shown by simulation, at lesser cost, whether this objective was feasible. This was certainly true, but the simulation approach left something to be desired in terms of a convincing demonstration. The real conflict that existed at this juncture was not whether simulation should precede field demonstration (which was agreed to by all parties), but rather whether the field demonstration would ever be justified (at a cost an order-of-magnitude greater than SOFT). The prevailing attitude in the Pentagon was that the experiment's objectives—essentially the execution of well-known guidance laws—were too straightforward to justify a costly experiment. This conflict, which had merit on both sides, is seen over and over again in major BMD ventures. When is it justified to commit to an expensive field experiment? When is a field experiment legitimately subject to the criticism that it lacks scientific merit, that it is a "stunt"?

In any event, HOE was delayed for about four years while high fidelity simulations were carried out to determine if exoatmospheric nonnuclear intercepts were feasible. The answer kept coming out "yes," with ever increasing confidence. (I do not cite this delay to make the point that it was a waste of time; given the indifferent political environment at the time the first approval was requested, it is probably just as well the delay was incurred).

HOE took about seven years from start to first flight, during which all of the classical symptoms of age for such programs were in evidence. Several times it was in danger of cancellation; for the last two or three years before its first flight, it suffered chronic budgetary malnutrition. HOE was a bold, ambitious program. Despite earlier concern that it was too straightforward, it required significant technical advancements to reduce the concept to practice. Fortunately, it did not suffer the fate of SOFT in being reduced to one shot, because its first shot was a failure. So was the second shot, and the third shot. The base of support for the program shrank with every failed flight, and ominous clouds of skepticism gathered to make its continuation uncertain. The fourth flight was a resounding success, resulting in the spectacular destruction of an ICBM warhead over the Pacific near Kwajalein Missile Range. Coming in the second year of the SDI program, the timing could not have been better. No program has ever received more favorable publicity than HOE.

Again, many different inferences could be drawn from the HOE experience. The trite observation that "all's well that ends well" is appropriate. More to the point, the essential quality of long-term support for the success of such major experiments can be clearly seen in the HOE example. There needs to be a sustained commitment, durable enough to survive changes in administrations, key players, and the political environment. This is not to say that there are not developments that may justify the termination of programs—such as arms control agreements—but the erosion of support due to impatience or shifting fads should not be a reason for termination. Having said all these good words, I confess that I do not know how to bring about such long-term program stability. I hope the right formula can be found for SDI. With its even more distant horizons, stability is more important than ever before.

In the two examples I have cited, SOFT and HOE, the programs did make it through to completion, despite their dark moments. There are many other examples where programs did not survive because of the vagaries of the "system." The Forward Acquisition System (FAS) is an example of a very forward-looking technology program canceled because of shifting political winds. The LoAD/Sentry program was canceled because it did not fit the criteria for advanced SDI development. Yet it is precisely the kind of system that needs to be restored in the program, with some modification, as a rapid deployment hedge.

In sharp contrast, the Soviet Union does not face the problem of program instability. A striking characteristic of their BMD program over the years is the continuity, persistence, and durability of their major program elements. I mentioned earlier that they have stuck with their Moscow system, in its various versions, for about thirty years. The ABM-X-3 program and others exhibit similar staying power. Obviously, they do not have the large number of players which engage in all large U.S. defense programs. They do not have so many reviewers with veto power. This has been cited as a disadvantage to the Soviets in some cases; and, indeed, I have seen isolated examples where it appears they would have benefited from dropping a program. But in BMD development, persistence is generally a huge advantage.

As with so many of the Soviet weapons development programs, their BMD programs have been characterized by high-longevity design teams. These teams progress incrementally from one generation of systems to the next with small, digestible bites of technology in between. They also take leaps into very exotic systems, but not at the expense of a solid base of evolving systems. The protracted development history of the Moscow system offers a case in point: once clearly inferior to Safeguard technology, it has been constantly upgraded so that it now represents a relatively sophisticated, layered defense system.

The Longevity of System Development Teams

In a similar manner, the progress of a number of U.S. BMD development teams in the past was marked by incremental improvements from one system generation to the next, not quantum leaps. This seems to hold true for many large-scale development enterprises, such as the Von Braun team's evolution from the Redstone missile to the Jupiter missile, and finally to the Saturn vehicles that propelled man to the moon.

The role of U.S. BMD teams was recognized by the physicist Freeman Dyson. Senator Moynihan, in his work cited earlier, has quoted an apt excerpt from Dyson's memoir, *Disturbing the Universe*:

The intellectual arrogance of my profession must take a large share of the blame [for not building defenses]. Defensive weapons do not spring, like the hydrogen bomb, from the brains of brilliant professors of physics. Defensive weapons are developed laboriously by teams of engineers in industrial laboratories.[56]

As indicated above, it is historically true that both U.S. and Soviet defense systems were developed and built by teams of engineers that worked together over a long period. This was nowhere more vividly demonstrated than in the large, resourceful BTL/Western Electric team during the Nike-Zeus, Nike-X, Sentinel, and Safeguard era of U.S. BMD development. It was also true during the era of Site Defense and LoAD/Sentry, under the leadership of the McDonnell Douglas team. In a slightly different sense, it was also a tribute to a persevering team centered at Lockheed and at the BMD Systems Command in Huntsville that the Homing Overlay Experiment (HOE) was successfully carried out. While HOE was an experiment rather than an integrated system development, its experimental objective required the same kind of protracted team effort as does a system development program.

The Interaction of System Development and Advanced Technology

While it is important to maintain large design teams to carry out BMD system development, it is also necessary to maintain laboratories for research and to devise mechanisms for interaction between the two. I have emphasized previously that a balance between long-term research and near-term development is an ideal to be sought in the SDI program. What I have not discussed is the interaction between the two, which is needed to infuse new technology into ongoing system development programs and to provide direction to advanced technology programs.

There are various degrees of "freezing" to which system development programs can be subjected, which determine how adaptable they are to new technology. During the Safeguard era, the mainstream development and deployment objectives were given such high priority that the system was not very adaptable to new technology. The Safeguard design was subjected to a "hard freeze." There are understandable reasons for this

---

[56] Moynihan, op. cit., p. 15.

happening on major deployment programs, not the least of which is that the program manager is judged mainly on how well he meets schedule and cost objectives. He is not judged as much on how technically up to date the system remains over the period of its development. This was not a serious problem on Safeguard; it had a relatively short deployment period, and its principal design features did not suffer a high degree of obsolescence during this period. However, there were advanced BMD technologies emerging from the parallel Advanced Technology Program—such as discrimination techniques—that could have enhanced Safeguard effectiveness.

The optimum balance between the extremes of freezing a system design to any infusion of new technology and leaving it open to continuous modification is difficult to achieve. A lot depends on how critical the end deployment date is. In many ways, the balance between the Site Defense and LoAD/Sentry systems and the ongoing advanced development program was about right, given that these systems were not subject to a critical end deployment date. On Site Defense, for example, there was continuous infusion of new technology that did not cause major system "breakage," and there were planned "block changes" for future upgrades. Discrimination algorithms coming out of advanced technology programs were picked up and incorporated into the Site Defense design. Major technology components, such as an advanced digital signal processor and an optical adjunct, were planned as upgrades to Site Defense subsequent to its initial prototype testing.

In the current SDI program, the problem of striking the right balance between frozen system designs and adaptability to new technology does not exist. Essentially, the entire program is dedicated to advanced technology. However, if a near-term system development program is adopted, such as the development of prototype terminal defense systems advocated in this study, then the mechanisms for technology transfer must be defined.

The major evolutionary steps for near-term system development were spelled out earlier in this study: first, develop a versatile terminal defense system that could be deployed rapidly; second, follow up with a midcourse overlay. These are the same two steps for both ATBM and CONUS application, the main difference being that the ATBM deployment would be treaty-compliant. The midcourse overlay could be available concurrently with (or only slightly later than) the terminal system if early derivatives of the ERIS and AOA components were selected rather than waiting for their full development. However, it does not appear that such early derivatives could be deployed for ATBM because of treaty issues.

Beyond the major evolutionary steps, a carefully structured development approach for the prototype terminal system would have to be worked out. Based on past experience, it would be most efficient to establish a prime contractor team with considerable autonomy, a long-term contract, and strong incentives to work on schedule. The major technical challenge faced by such a system is nonnuclear kill; therefore, provisions would have to be made to accommodate new technology bearing on this critical issue. Ideally, the baseline approach for the guidance mechanization for nonnuclear kill could be confidently selected following concept definition, so that subsequent technology transfer would be more at the component level—such as improved inertial measurement unit (IMU) and fuze designs.

The most important factor for the success of a near-term system development initiative is that the development team be shielded from disruptive day-to-day changes in direction. If the quality of the accelerated development effort on a terminal system is to be commensurate with its national urgency, it must be performed in such an environment.

PERGAMON-BRASSEY'S
International Defense Publishers

List of Publications
published for the
Institute for Foreign Policy Analysis, Inc.

Orders for the following titles should be addressed to: Pergamon-Brassey's, Maxwell House, Fairview Park, Elmsford, New York, 10523; or to Pergamon-Brassey's, Headington Hill Hall, Oxford, OX3 0BW, England.

Foreign Policy Reports

ETHICS,DETERRENCE, AND NATIONAL SECURITY. By James E. Dougherty, Midge Decter, Pierre Hassner, Laurence Martin, Michael Novak, and Vladimir Bukovsky. June 1985. xvi, 91pp. $9.95.

AMERICAN SEA POWER AND GLOBAL STRATEGY. By Robert J. Hanks. October 1985. viii, 92pp. $9.95.

DECISION-MAKING IN COMMUNIST COUNTRIES: AN INSIDE VIEW. By Jan Sejna and Joseph D. Douglass, Jr. 1986. xii, 75pp. $9.95.

NATIONAL SECURITY: ETHICS, STRATEGY, AND POLITICS. A LAYMAN'S PRIMER. By Robert L. Pfaltzgraff, Jr. 1986. v, 37pp. $9.95.

DETERRING CHEMICAL WARFARE: U.S. POLICY OPTIONS FOR THE 1990S. By Hugh Stringer. 1986. xii, 71pp. $9.95.

THE CRISIS OF COMMUNISM: ITS MEANING, ORIGINS, AND PHASES. By Rett R. Ludwikowski. 1986. xii, 78pp. $9.95.

Special Reports

STRATEGIC MINERALS AND INTERNATIONAL SECURITY. Edited by Uri Ra'anan and Charles M. Perry. July 1985. viii, 85pp. $9.95.

THIRD WORLD MARXIST-LENINIST REGIMES: STRENGTHS, VULNERABILITIES, AND U.S. POLICY. By Uri Ra'anan, Francis Fukuyama, Mark Falcoff, Sam C. Sarkesian, and Richard H. Shultz, Jr. September 1985. xv, 125pp. $9.95.

THE RED ARMY ON PAKISTAN'S BORDER: POLICY IMPLICATIONS FOR THE UNITED STATES. By Anthony Arnold, Richard P. Cronin, Thomas Perry Thornton, Theodore L. Eliot, Jr., and Robert L. Pfaltzgraff, Jr. 1986. vi, 82pp. $9.95.

Books

ATLANTIC COMMUNITY IN CRISIS: A REDEFINITION OF THE ATLANTIC RELATIONSHIP. Edited by Walter F. Hahn and Robert L. Pfaltzgraff, Jr. 1979. 386pp. $43.00.

REVISING U.S. MILITARY STRATEGY: TAILORING MEANS TO ENDS. By Jeffrey Record. 1984. 113pp. $16.95 ($9.95, paper).

SHATTERING EUROPE'S DEFENSE CONSENSUS: THE ANTINUCLEAR PROTEST MOVEMENT AND THE FUTURE OF NATO. Edited by James E. Dougherty and Robert L. Pfaltzgraff, Jr. 1985. 226pp. $18.95.

INSTITUTE FOR FOREIGN POLICY ANALYSIS, INC.
List of Publications

Orders for the following titles in IFPA's series of Special Reports, Foreign Policy Reports, National Security Papers, Conference Reports, and Books should be addressed to the Circulation Manager, Institute for Foreign Policy Analysis, Central Plaza Building, Tenth Floor, 675 Massachusetts Avenue, Cambridge, Massachusetts 02139-3396. (Telephone: 617-492-2116.) Please send a check or money order for the correct amount together with your order.

Foreign Policy Reports

DEFENSE TECHNOLOGY AND THE ATLANTIC ALLIANCE: COMPETITION OR COLLABORATION? By Frank T.J. Bray and Michael Moodie. April 1977. vi, 42pp. $5.00.

IRAN'S QUEST FOR SECURITY: U.S. ARMS TRANSFERS AND THE NUCLEAR OPTION. By Alvin J. Cottrell and James E. Dougherty. May 1977. 59pp. $5.00.

ETHIOPIA, THE HORN OF AFRICA, AND U.S. POLICY. By John H. Spencer. September 1977. 69pp. $5.00.

BEYOND THE ARAB-ISRAELI SETTLEMENT: NEW DIRECTIONS FOR U.S. POLICY IN THE MIDDLE EAST. By R.K. Ramazani. September 1977. viii, 69pp. $5.00.

SPAIN, THE MONARCHY AND THE ATLANTIC COMMUNITY. By David C. Jordan. June 1979. v, 55pp. $5.00.

U.S. STRATEGY AT THE CROSSROADS: TWO VIEWS. By Robert J. Hanks and Jeffrey Record. July 1982. viii, 69pp. $7.50.

THE U.S. MILITARY PRESENCE IN THE MIDDLE EAST: PROBLEMS AND PROSPECTS. By Robert J. Hanks. December 1982. vii, 77pp. $7.50.

SOUTHERN AFRICA AND WESTERN SECURITY. By Robert J. Hanks. August 1983. vii, 71pp. $7.50.

THE WEST GERMAN PEACE MOVEMENT AND THE NATIONAL QUESTION. By Kim R. Holmes. March 1984. x, 73pp. $7.50.

THE HISTORY AND IMPACT OF MARXIST-LENINIST ORGANIZATIONAL THEORY. By John P. Roche. April 1984. x, 70pp. $7.50.

Special Reports

THE CRUISE MISSILE: BARGAINING CHIP OR DEFENSE BARGAIN? By Robert L. Pfaltzgraff, Jr., and Jacquelyn K. Davis. January 1977. x, 53pp. $3.00.

EUROCOMMUNISM AND THE ATLANTIC ALLIANCE. By James E. Dougherty and Diane K. Pfaltzgraff. January 1977. xiv, 66pp. $3.00.

THE NEUTRON BOMB: POLITICAL, TECHNICAL, AND MILITARY ISSUES. By S.T. Cohen. November 1978. xii, 95pp. $6.50.

SALT II AND U.S.-SOVIET STRATEGIC FORCES. By Jacquelyn K. Davis, Patrick J. Friel, and Robert L. Pfaltzgraff, Jr. June 1979. xii, 51pp. $5.00.

THE EMERGING STRATEGIC ENVIRONMENT: IMPLICATIONS FOR BALLISTIC MISSILE DEFENSE. By Leon Gouré, William G. Hyland, and Colin S. Gray. December 1979. xi, 75pp. $6.50.

THE SOVIET UNION AND BALLISTIC MISSILE DEFENSE. By Jacquelyn K. Davis, Uri Ra'anan, Robert L. Pfaltzgraff, Jr., Michael J. Deane, and John M. Collins. March 1980. xi, 71pp. $6.50. (Out of print).

ENERGY ISSUES AND ALLIANCE RELATIONSHIPS: THE UNITED STATES, WESTERN EUROPE AND JAPAN. By Robert L. Pfaltzgraff, Jr. April 1980. xii, 71pp. $6.50.

U.S. STRATEGIC-NUCLEAR POLICY AND BALLISTIC MISSILE DEFENSE: THE 1980S AND BEYOND. By William Schneider, Jr., Donald G. Brennan, William A. Davis, Jr., and Hans Rühle. April 1980. xii, 61pp. $6.50.

THE UNNOTICED CHALLENGE: SOVIET MARITIME STRATEGY AND THE GLOBAL CHOKE POINTS. By Robert J. Hanks. August 1980. xi, 66pp. $6.50.

FORCE REDUCTIONS IN EUROPE: STARTING OVER. By Jeffrey Record. October 1980. xi, 91pp. $6.50.

SALT II AND AMERICAN SECURITY. By Gordon J. Humphrey, William R. Van Cleave, Jeffrey Record, William H. Kincade, and Richard Perle. October 1980. xvi, 65pp.

THE FUTURE OF U.S. LAND-BASED STRATEGIC FORCES. By Jake Garn, J.I. Coffey, Lord Chalfont, and Ellery B. Block. December 1980. xvi, 80pp.

THE CAPE ROUTE: IMPERILED WESTERN LIFELINE. By Robert J. Hanks. February 1981. xi, 80pp. $6.50. (Hardcover, $10.00).

POWER PROJECTION AND THE LONG-RANGE COMBAT AIRCRAFT: MISSIONS, CAPABILITIES AND ALTERNATIVE DESIGNS. By Jacquelyn K. Davis and Robert L. Pfaltzgraff, Jr. June 1981. ix, 37pp. $6.50.

THE PACIFIC FAR EAST: ENDANGERED AMERICAN STRATEGIC POSITION. By Robert J. Hanks. October 1981. vii, 75pp. $7.50.

NATO'S THEATER NUCLEAR FORCE MODERNIZATION PROGRAM: THE REAL ISSUES. By Jeffrey Record. November 1981. viii, 102pp. $7.50.

THE CHEMISTRY OF DEFEAT: ASYMMETRIES IN U.S. AND SOVIET CHEMICAL WARFARE POSTURES. By Amoretta M. Hoeber. December 1981. xiii, 91pp. $6.50.

THE HORN OF AFRICA: A MAP OF POLITICAL-STRATEGIC CONFLICT. By James E. Dougherty. April 1982. xv, 74pp. $7.50.

THE WEST, JAPAN AND CAPE ROUTE IMPORTS: THE OIL AND NON-FUEL MINERAL TRADES. By Charles Perry. June 1982. xiv, 88pp. $7.50.

THE RAPID DEPLOYMENT FORCE AND U.S. MILITARY INTERVENTION IN THE PERSIAN GULF. By Jeffrey Record. May 1983, Second Edition. viii, 83pp. $7.50.

THE GREENS OF WEST GERMANY: ORIGINS, STRATEGIES, AND TRANSATLANTIC IMPLICATIONS. By Robert L. Pfaltzgraff, Jr., Kim R. Holmes, Clay Clemens, and Werner Kaltefleiter. August 1983. xi, 105pp. $7.50.

THE ATLANTIC ALLIANCE AND U.S. GLOBAL STRATEGY. By Jacquelyn K. Davis and Robert L. Pfaltzgraff, Jr. September 1983. x, 44pp. $7.50.

WORLD ENERGY SUPPLY AND INTERNATIONAL SECURITY. By Herman Franssen, John P. Hardt, Jacquelyn K. Davis, Robert J. Hanks, Charles Perry, Robert L. Pfaltzgraff, Jr., and Jeffrey Record. October 1983. xiv, 93pp. $7.50.

POISONING ARMS CONTROL: THE SOVIET UNION AND CHEMICAL/BIOLOGICAL WEAPONS. By Mark C. Storella. June 1984. xi, 99pp. $7.50.

National Security Papers

CBW: THE POOR MAN'S ATOMIC BOMB. By Neil C. Livingstone and Joseph D. Douglass, Jr., with a Foreword by Senator John Tower. February 1984. x, 33pp. $5.00.

U.S. STRATEGIC AIRLIFT: REQUIREMENTS AND CAPABILITIES. By Jeffrey Record. January 1986. vi, 38pp. $6.00.

STRATEGIC BOMBERS: HOW MANY ARE ENOUGH? By Jeffrey Record. January 1986. vi, 22pp. $6.00.

STRATEGIC DEFENSE AND EXTENDED DETERRENCE: A NEW TRANSATLANTIC DEBATE. By Jacquelyn K. Davis and Robert L. Pfaltzgraff, Jr. February 1986. viii, 53pp. $8.00.

JCS REORGANIZATION AND U.S. ARMS CONTROL POLICY. By James E. Dougherty. March 1986. xiv, 27pp. $6.00.

STRATEGIC FORCE MODERNIZATION AND ARMS CONTROL. Contributions by Edward L. Rowny, R. James Woolsey, Harold Brown, Alexander M. Haig, Jr., Albert Gore, Jr., Brent Scowcroft, Russell E. Dougherty, A. Casey, Gordon Fornell, and Sam Nunn. 1986. xi, 43pp. $6.00.

Books

SOVIET MILITARY STRATEGY IN EUROPE. By Joseph D. Douglass, Jr. Pergamon Press, 1980. 252pp. (Out of print).

THE WARSAW PACT: ARMS, DOCTRINE, AND STRATEGY. By William J. Lewis. New York: McGraw-Hill Publishing Co., 1982. 471pp. $15.00.

THE BISHOPS AND NUCLEAR WEAPONS: THE CATHOLIC PASTORAL LETTER ON WAR AND PEACE. By James E. Dougherty. Archon Books, 1984. 255pp. $22.50.

Conference Reports

NATO AND ITS FUTURE: A GERMAN-AMERICAN ROUNDTABLE. Summary of a Dialogue. 1978. 22pp. $1.00.

SECOND GERMAN-AMERICAN ROUNDTABLE ON NATO: THE THEATER-NUCLEAR BALANCE. 1978. 32pp. $1.00.

THE SOVIET UNION AND BALLISTIC MISSILE DEFENSE. 1978. 26pp. $1.00.

U.S. STRATEGIC-NUCLEAR POLICY AND BALLISTIC MISSILE DEFENSE: THE 1980S AND BEYOND. 1979. 30pp. $1.00.

SALT II AND AMERICAN SECURITY. 1979. 39pp.

THE FUTURE OF U.S. LAND-BASED STRATEGIC FORCES. 1979. 32pp.

THE FUTURE OF NUCLEAR POWER. 1980. 48pp. $1.00.

THIRD GERMAN-AMERICAN ROUNDTABLE ON NATO: MUTUAL AND BALANCED FORCE REDUCTIONS IN EUROPE. 1980. 27pp. $1.00.

FOURTH GERMAN-AMERICAN ROUNDTABLE ON NATO: NATO MODERNIZATION AND EUROPEAN SECURITY. 1981. 15pp. $1.00.

SECOND ANGLO-AMERICAN SYMPOSIUM ON DETERRENCE AND EUROPEAN SECURITY. 1981. 25pp. $1.00.

THE U.S. DEFENSE MOBILIZATION INFRASTRUCTURE: PROBLEMS AND PRIORITIES. The Tenth Annual Conference, sponsored by the International Security Studies Program, The Fletcher School of Law and Diplomacy, Tufts University. 1981. 25pp. $1.00.

U.S. STRATEGIC DOCTRINE FOR THE 1980S. 1982. 14pp.

FRENCH-AMERICAN SYMPOSIUM ON STRATEGY, DETERRENCE AND EUROPEAN SECURITY. 1982. 14pp. $1.00.

FIFTH GERMAN-AMERICAN ROUNDTABLE ON NATO: THE CHANGING CONTEXT OF THE EUROPEAN SECURITY DEBATE. Summary of a Transatlantic Dialogue. 1982. 22pp. $1.00.

ENERGY SECURITY AND THE FUTURE OF NUCLEAR POWER. 1982. 39pp. $2.50.

INTERNATIONAL SECURITY DIMENSIONS OF SPACE. The Eleventh Annual Conference, sponsored by the International Security Studies Program, The Fletcher School of Law and Diplomacy, Tufts University. 1982. 24pp. $2.50.

PORTUGAL, SPAIN AND TRANSATLANTIC RELATIONS. Summary of a Transatlantic Dialogue. 1983. 18pp. $2.50.

JAPANESE-AMERICAN SYMPOSIUM ON REDUCING STRATEGIC MINERALS VULNERABILITIES: CURRENT PLANS, PRIORITIES, AND POSSIBILITIES FOR COOPERATION. 1983. 31pp. $2.50.

NATIONAL SECURITY POLICY: THE DECISION-MAKING PROCESS. The Twelfth Annual Conference, sponsored by the International Security Studies Program, The Fletcher School of Law and Diplomacy, Tufts University. 1983. 28pp. $2.50.

THE SECURITY OF THE ATLANTIC, IBERIAN AND NORTH AFRICAN REGIONS. Summary of a Transatlantic Dialogue. 1983. 25pp. $2.50.

THE WEST EUROPEAN ANTINUCLEAR PROTEST MOVEMENT: IMPLICATIONS FOR WESTERN SECURITY. Summary of a Transatlantic Dialogue. 1984. 21pp. $2.50.

THE U.S.-JAPANESE SECURITY RELATIONSHIP IN TRANSITION. Summary of a Transpacific Dialogue. 1984. 23pp. $2.50.

SIXTH GERMAN-AMERICAN ROUNDTABLE ON NATO: NATO AND EUROPEAN SECURITY—BEYOND INF. Summary of a Transatlantic Dialogue. 1984. 31pp. $2.50.

SECURITY COMMITMENTS AND CAPABILITIES: ELEMENTS OF AN AMERICAN GLOBAL STRATEGY. The Thirteenth Annual Conference, sponsored by the International Security Studies Program, The Fletcher School of Law and Diplomacy, Tufts University. 1984. 21pp. $2.50.

THIRD JAPANESE-AMERICAN-GERMAN CONFERENCE ON THE FUTURE OF NUCLEAR ENERGY. 1984. 40pp. $2.50.

SEVENTH GERMAN-AMERICAN ROUNDTABLE ON NATO: POLITICAL CONSTRAINTS, EMERGING TECHNOLOGIES, AND ALLIANCE STRATEGY. Summary of a Transatlantic Dialogue. 1985. 36pp. $2.50.

TERRORISM AND OTHER "LOW-INTENSITY" OPERATIONS: INTERNATIONAL LINKAGES. The Fourteenth Annual Conference, sponsored by the International Security Studies Program, The Fletcher School of Law and Diplomacy, Tufts University. 1985. 21pp. $2.50.

EAST-WEST TRADE AND TECHNOLOGY TRANSFER: NEW CHALLENGES FOR THE UNITED STATES. Second Annual Forum, co-sponsored by the Institute for Foreign Policy Analysis and the International Security Studies Program, The Fletcher School of Law and Diplomacy, Tufts University. 1986. 40pp. $3.50.

ORGANIZING FOR NATIONAL SECURITY: THE ROLE OF THE JOINT CHIEFS OF STAFF. 1986. 32pp. $2.50.

EIGHTH GERMAN-AMERICAN ROUNDTABLE ON NATO: STRATEGIC DEFENSE, NATO MODERNIZATION, AND EAST-WEST RELATIONS. Summary of a Transatlantic Dialogue. 1986. 47pp. $2.50.

EMERGING DOCTRINES AND TECHNOLOGIES: IMPLICATIONS FOR GLOBAL AND REGIONAL POLITICAL-MILITARY BALANCES. The Fifteenth Annual Conference, sponsored by the International Security Studies Program, The Fletcher School of Law and Diplomacy, Tufts University. 1986. 49pp. $2.50.

STRATEGIC WAR TERMINATION: POLITICAL-MILITARY-DIPLOMATIC DIMENSIONS. 1986. 22pp. $2.50.

40 006